FRANK HACKETT-JONES

1892–1988

FRANK HACKETT-JONES

1892–1988

A 20th-century Australian Life

DON CHAMBERS

HYLAND HOUSE PUBLISHING

First published in Australia in 2008 by
Hyland House Publishing Pty Ltd
PO Box 122
Flemington, Victoria 3031

National Library of Australia Cataloguing-in-Publication entry

Author: Chambers, Don (Donald), 1935-
Title: Frank Hackett-Jones 1892-1988 : a 20th century
           Australian life / Don Chambers.
ISBN: 9781864471120 (hbk.)
Notes: Includes index. Bibliography.
Subjects: Hackett-Jones, Frank, 1892-1988.
           Civil service – New South Wales – Biography.
           Farmers – New South Wales – Canowindra – Biography.
           Christian biography – Australia.
           Australia – History – 20th century – Biography.
Dewey
Number: 994.04092

Edited by Martin P. Schoo
Layout and design by Pauline Deakin, Captured Concepts
Printed by Everbest, China

Foreword

He was a deep thinker, a reader, a man of contemplative nature, somewhat on the fringes of society. Through his many evolutions, as son-of-a-clergyman, accountant, public servant, soldier, barrister, farmer, husband, and father of six, Frank Hackett-Jones lived a conscientious life, driven by an acute sense of social responsibility and a desire for justice.

In 1983, my brother Frank commissioned this biography from Historian Dr Don Chambers, who interviewed our father over a week, and brought his knowledge of Australian and Church history to bear on everything from our father's enigmatic, possibly convict roots, to his wartime experiences, his farming years in flood-prone NSW, and his later retirement to Adelaide. By the time of his death, in January 1988, our father had participated in nearly a century of Australian life.

We thank Don Chambers for his ability to get alongside of a man who was not prone to yarn or tell stories. In doing this, he has managed to enlarge our knowledge of the many experiences we were not part of.

This book is dedicated to the memory of our father, Frank, a man whom we were graced to be a part of, and to our brother, Frank Jr, who died at 58 years of age in 2000. They live on in our lives.

Jennie Hackett
Adelaide, April 2008

Acknowledgements

This work was commissioned by Frank Hackett-Jones' eldest son, Frank, founder of Telspec PLC, UK.

Due to Don Chambers' intimate knowledge of both Australian and Church history, it has become both a cherished portrait of our father and a valuable document of Australian social history.

Contents

Hackett-Jones Family Tree (simplified)

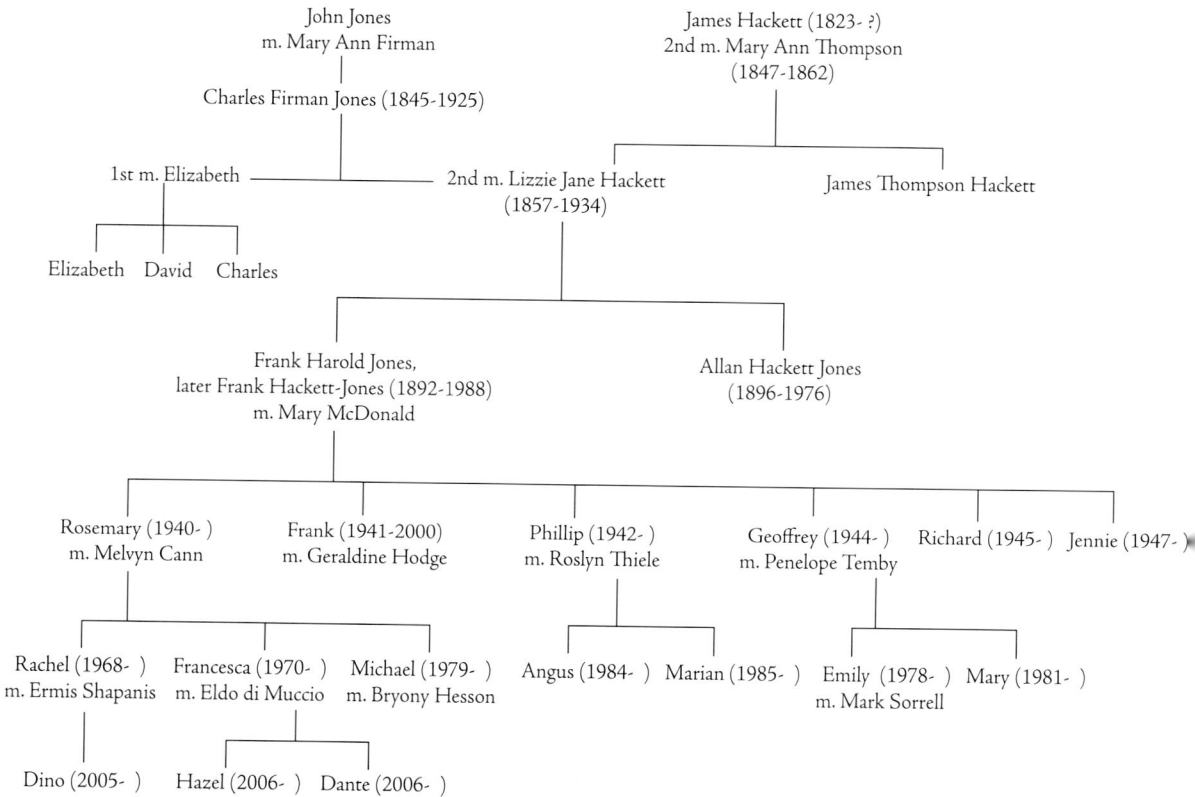

John Jones
m. Mary Ann Firman

James Hackett (1823- ?)
2nd m. Mary Ann Thompson
(1847-1862)

Charles Firman Jones (1845-1925)

1st m. Elizabeth

2nd m. Lizzie Jane Hackett
(1857-1934)

James Thompson Hackett

Elizabeth   David   Charles

Frank Harold Jones,
later Frank Hackett-Jones (1892-1988)
m. Mary McDonald

Allan Hackett Jones
(1896-1976)

Rosemary (1940-)
m. Melvyn Cann

Frank (1941-2000)
m. Geraldine Hodge

Phillip (1942-)
m. Roslyn Thiele

Geoffrey (1944-)
m. Penelope Temby

Richard (1945-)   Jennie (1947-)

Rachel (1968-)
m. Ermis Shapanis

Francesca (1970-)
m. Eldo di Muccio

Michael (1979-)
m. Bryony Hesson

Angus (1984-)   Marian (1985-)

Emily (1978-)
m. Mark Sorrell

Mary (1981-)

Dino (2005-)

Hazel (2006-)   Dante (2006-)

ANCESTORS

Frank Harold Jones was born near Botany Bay on 9 July 1892, and died as Frank Harold Hackett-Jones at Adelaide on 18 January 1988. He had a deep interest in history and tradition, and over a long lifetime had (with his brother Allan) assembled a considerable amount of basic information about his immediate paternal and maternal ancestry. He was conscious that his father's Jones ancestral line was of humble and obscure origins, whereas his mother's Hackett ancestry stemmed from a more socially substantial and well-educated Irish gentry background.

Frank Hackett-Jones' own father, the long-serving New South Wales Methodist minister Rev. Charles Firman Jones, said that he had been born at Parramatta on 6 December, 1844 to John Jones and Mary Ann Firman. That parental union remains mysterious, and we cannot assume that John Jones and Mary Ann Firman were legally married. Given that their son seems never to have known his parents, and that he was brought up by strangers in another colony far from his place of origin, his birth might have been the product of a fleeting liaison. Marriage was a state that was frequently taken lightly in the convict colony of New South Wales. John Jones was described by his grandson as having been a goldbeater and an innkeeper, in a society still heavily weighted to people of a convict background with a hankering after crude and cheap alcoholic spirits, and the son was born in a Parramatta district infamous for its convict Female Factory.

On Rev. Charles Firman Jones' marriage and death certificates his father was described as a 'goldbeater', without any reference to innkeeping. It would appear that the innkeeping

Charles Firman Jones, Elizabeth Emily Louise Jones, James Hackett, Adelaide Hackett and Lizzie Jane Jones (née Hackett)

background was kept a secret within the Jones family, but that 'innkeeper' description was no invention of John Jones' descendants. On 29 December 1844 Charles Jones was baptised in St John's Anglican parish church at Parramatta. His father was described as John Jones, and his mother simply as Mary, and the father's occupation was given as innkeeper. There was no mention of Firman either in relation to the child's second name, or in relation to its mother's identity. This baptismal record might suggest that the minister who baptised the child believed its parents to be legally married: it is the only indication that we have of such a conventional marriage situation. However, in my own convict ancestry there are several instances where the children of de facto parents were baptised by Anglican clergy in early New South Wales, without comment.

It is easy to understand why a respected Methodist minister being married in a Methodist Church would not insert 'innkeeper' as his father's occupation on his own marriage certificate. On the other hand, it is unlikely that such a person, if he were inventing an occupation for a father whom he never knew, would choose goldbeater. A less likely occupation in early New South Wales would be difficult to contemplate. There would have been precious few gold ingots to beat into gold leaf in New South Wales around 1840, and few buyers for the finished product, so John Jones would most probably have been an innkeeper during his colonial phase as Charles Jones' baptism record suggests. That innkeeping background was no source of pride to the family of a later 19th-century Methodist parsonage, nor did Frank Hackett-Jones appear impressed by it. The mystery and dubiousness of his personal origins had doubtless deeply affected the developing personality of the young Charles Firman Jones, and probably contributed to his extreme quietness in most social situations, as also to his dogged commitment to the vocation of a Methodist minister. Something of the father's reticence in ordinary social communication would be passed on to Frank Hackett-Jones. Small talk would never be his strong point.

The vocations of goldbeater and innkeeper in early colonial New South Wales appear highly suspect. Anyone beating gold in England at that time was not unlikely to have been tempted to become a receiver of stolen goods. Why would a goldbeater voluntarily have come to Parramatta in the 1830s or 1840s, when there was no Australian gold to beat? A favourite role for an ex-convict was that of innkeeper, because such men knew the power of cheap and potent rum in the colonies. It appears highly likely that John Jones was himself of convict origins, and perhaps Mary Ann Firman also. The name 'John Jones' was so common that Frank Hackett-Jones' grandfather could prove very difficult to isolate in early New South Wales records. The New South Wales census of 1828 listed over sixty persons of that name, most being of convict background. Apart from the extremely common occurrence of both segments of the name, what could be more suitable as an alias for an ex-convict desiring anonymity in a convict colony, than the label 'John Jones'? The mother's name of Mary Ann Firman might be thought easier to trace.

The surname Firman was not uncommon in Suffolk around the time that Charles Firman Jones was born at Parramatta. One of his sons, using England's Somerset House records, was able to find two young Suffolk ladies of the name Mary Ann (or Mary Anne) Firman, each of whom was married to a village labourer in England during the years 1844-1845. However, it would appear extremely unlikely that either of these nineteen-year-old girls mothered Charles

Firman Jones at Parramatta on 6 December 1844. An illiterate servant girl named Mary Anne (not Mary Ann) Firman was married to one James Webb at the parish church of Erigwell, Suffolk, on 4 February 1844. She is most unlikely to have mothered a son for a John Jones at distant Parramatta in December of that same year. Even had she run sufficiently foul of English law soon after her marriage to justify transportation, the legal processes would hardly have allowed such rapid transit to the Antipodes. There is also the problem of the 'Anne' rather than 'Ann', and the fact that she would have been unlikely to revert to her maiden name in Australia. On the 8 February 1845, another spinster named Mary Ann Firman married a labourer named William Nunn at Wortham in County Suffolk. Given sailing-ship schedules of that day, it is even less likely that such a young spinster could have returned to Suffolk to marry, after having given birth to Charles Firman Jones at Parramatta only three months previously.[1]

The Joneses

One John Jones (not surprisingly) did appear in Lloyd Robson's book, *The Convict Settlers of Australia*. This man was listed as belonging to the Middlesex Gaol Delivery of 21 April 1819, and he was shipped on the *Eliza* in 1819. John Jones, assigned servant to D. Macintyre, stopped reaping too long before breakfast and was awarded fifty lashes for impertinence to the overseer. Robson's information came from records of the Hunter River Bench, 1831-32. That unfortunate man was one of very many convicts who used the name John Jones in early New South Wales, and he was certainly not Frank Hackett-Jones' ancestor. The system of 'assigning' convict servants was stopped in 1842. Work became difficult to obtain in a period of extreme economic depression, and many an 'old lag' went off in search of an inn to run at about that time – that is, just before Charles Firman Jones was born at Parramatta.[2]

The full scope of the New South Wales 'John Jones problem' can only fully be appreciated when we approach the detailed convict 'indent' records, covering all those unfortunates shipped in the direction of Botany Bay between 1788 and 1842. The indexes to the wonderful modern microfiche copies of those historic registers list more than two hundred different references to convicts using the name John Jones, all of whom came to New South Wales in those years. A few of those entries duplicate references to the same individual. Doubtless, many others with the name 'John Jones' went to Van Diemen's Land, and there was always the possibility that such men might ultimately find their way to New South Wales to complicate the problem of finding a goldbeater named John Jones. However, it is most unlikely that Van Diemonian ex-convicts of that name had wandered into the Parramatta district by the early 1840s, when Charles Firman Jones was born.[3]

Few of those numerous New South Wales convicts named John Jones, whose details have been pursued in the indent records, were guilty of crimes of violence or crimes against the person. Among the many convicts named John Jones who were transported to New South Wales between 1825 and 1842, the only person charged explicitly with a crime of violence was a twenty-year-old Roman Catholic hairdresser from Waterford who received a life sentence for rape. He was probably lucky not to hang. The next most violent crimes of a John Jones were a couple of cases of highway robbery, although the charges and sentences do not suggest that actual violence had been used on the King's Highway. We may assume that there had been other men of the name of John Jones who were involved in more violent crimes than most of those recorded in the New South Wales indents, but such men were probably hanged in their country of origin.

To put that rape sentence into perspective, we might note the case of the twenty-nine-year-old married Protestant John Jones from Stepney, described as a seaman and a paperhanger, who received a life sentence for stealing a Prayer Book and was duly transported to New South Wales in 1830. Admittedly, his record indicated two previous sentences, but whether those previous misdemeanours had also indicated an interest in religion the indents do not show. In 1843, having served about fourteen years of his sentence, this purloiner of Prayer Books was granted an absolute pardon by Governor George Gipps. He was not the only John Jones whose tangling with religion between 1825 and 1842 had earned him a free passage to New South Wales. A twenty-three-year-old Protestant widower from Hampshire, a shoemaker, found himself bouncing on the high seas in 1837 for having committed the crime of 'sacrilege'. Whether his crime also involved prayer books is unclear.

The great majority of those named John Jones in New South Wales (and that included the category 'John Jones alias Bill Smith' as well as the category 'Bill Smith alias John Jones') obtained their lengthy free passages for what appear to modern man to have been trivial misdemeanours. They came from all over England and Wales and Ireland, many of them pickpockets, some for stealing a handkerchief or a coat, some for stealing a fowl, a sheep, pigs, a horse, and in one case even a donkey. I only found one John Jones deported for practicing that honoured old English pastime of poaching. One unfortunate John Jones had been convicted of stealing 'a brass cock', another for stealing a hat, another for stealing a necklace, and yet another for stealing a dress pin. In looking for a goldbeater, one's eye might be caught by references to stealing gold, but for all indent entries perused for the period 1820 to 1842, there was not one reference to a John Jones stealing gold.

Convicts named John Jones were consigned to the Antipodes for stealing lead, for stealing brass, for creating 'base coin', for stealing silver plate, for stealing a ring – or a watch – that might conceivably have contained gold. But nowhere have I found an explicit reference to stolen gold. Probably, few men named John Jones lived in environments where gold was convenient for the plucking. I have found only one white-collar criminal bearing that ancient and honourable name. He was a mercantile clerk from Manchester who had also tried soldiery, and had been convicted of forgery at Calcutta. An occasional John Jones of military aspirations was transported for deserting the flag, in one case unsurprisingly while on the King's service in Dublin.

All of this points to one interesting fact about the ancestry of Rev. Charles Firman Jones, born at Parramatta in 1844. Insofar as he had a father who was a goldbeater, as Charles Firman Jones' wedding certificate and other documents indicated, then Frank Hackett-Jones' ancestry was a cut above the ordinary run of Joneses in New South Wales. Most of them would hardly have known what gold looked like. A search of the convict indents covering all those men named John Jones who were transported to New South Wales between 1820 and 1842 has not turned up one solitary individual whose occupation was described as 'goldbeater' in the official record. On the other hand, why would such a skilled craftsman as a goldbeater have been found at Parramatta in the early 1840s, unless sent there at the royal expense and pleasure?

The indents for that period do indicate a single John Jones whose occupation did involve workmanship in gold and silver. An individual of that name, aged thirty-nine years, Protestant and single, was described in the official record as 'gold- and silver-wire drawer'. His crime was not that of making free with his employer's gold or silver ingots, but one of 'stealing brass'. He was a Londoner, as were virtually all skilled English workers in gold and silver during the early 19th century; and he was listed as 'Middlesex Gaol Delivery' of 23 October 1830. He had no former convictions, which probably explains the relatively light sentence of seven years transportation. Standing five feet seven-and-a-half inches, his complexion was 'ruddy, freckled, and pock-pitted'. He had brown to grey hair, and brown eyes. Whether or not this man was the ancestor of Rev. Charles Firman Jones, it is almost certain that the 'goldbeater' father referred to on his marriage certificate would have hailed from the London area, and it is extremely unlikely that he came to Sydney of his own free will. Whoever actually fathered Charles Firman Jones in 1844 most probably had a life story not unlike that of this gold-wire drawer from London.

John Jones, the gold- and silver-wire drawer, had been tried at Middlesex on 28 March 1830, and sailed out of London on 1 April 1831 as one of 180 male prisoners aboard the *Georgiana* (Master, J.T. Thompson) bound for Port Jackson. This vessel of 403 tons, with its 29 soldiers of the 11th Light Dragoons and 16th Regiment of Foot to maintain order aboard, along with four soldiers' wives and one child, put into Port Jackson on 27 July 1831. That John Jones was more fortunate than a namesake aboard the *Georgiana*, a Manchester labourer who had received a life sentence at Lancaster in 1831. It was not uncommon to find more than one John Jones on a convict transport.

John Jones, the gold- and silver-wire drawer from London, received his ticket-of-leave, allowing him to move in search of work around the district of Sutton Forest in the County of Camden, on the recommendation of the Bong Bong Bench, in August 1836. The Londoner had apparently been assigned to a landowner in that pastoral district, most probably as a shepherd. His sentence should normally have expired within a year or two of that date. In fact, his Certificate of Freedom is dated 30 May 1840, and it indicates that this John Jones resided in the Berrima district, close to where he had received his ticket-of-leave in December 1836.[4]

There is nothing intrinsically improbable about this ex-convict having become an innkeeper by 1844. It is of interest to note that one of two licensed New South Wales innkeepers with the name John Jones operated at a coastal settlement not far from Sutton Forest and Berrima between September 1843 and June 1844, when he disappeared from the licensing records of that district. He did business at what (from the obscure handwriting of the Licence butt) appears to have been the South Huskisson Hotel at Jervis Bay. It is by no means impossible, or even improbable, that having found custom limited around Jervis Bay this man then moved to the relatively populous road-junction centre of Parramatta to increase his profits. The name John Jones certainly turned up among the licensed publicans of Parramatta in the immediately subsequent period, not having occurred there during the early 1840s.

It was difficult to run a hotel without female assistance, and willing female helpers for an ageing publican were more likely to be found in the vicinity of Parramatta than at Jervis Bay. He may even have moved to the more civilised environs of Parramatta in the knowledge that Mary Jones was already pregnant.[5]

We do not know on what basis Charles Firman Jones identified his father's occupation on later 19th-century official documents. Had the father whom he could not remember been the gold-wire drawer of the convict indents, it is not unlikely that goldbeater would have been the term to come most readily to his son's mind. A foster parent relying on memory would have difficulty in remembering gold-wire drawer. However, the trade of a goldbeater in London at that time implied a more highly valued skill than did that of a gold-wire drawer. A craftsman who carefully beat out bars of gold into gold leaf needed to be trustworthy, because gold leaf was easily purloined in small quantities, in ways that an employer might find difficult to pin down. A gold-wire drawer, on the other hand, had very little contact with large quantities of gold. Superior gold wire was gilded silver wire. In its cheaper forms (as for theatre use) it was gilded copper wire. In England during the 19th century gold wire was never what it claimed to be, and the amounts of gold used in the gilding process were minimal.

The production of gold or silver thread for weaving or embroidering was mainly carried on in India, where traditional methods were still used. In 19th-century India, as in medieval England, the production of gold wire for embroidery work had involved goldbeating:

> The wire is flattened into the strip or ribbon-like form it generally assumes by passing it, fourteen or fifteen strands simultaneously, over a fine, smooth round-topped anvil, and beating it as it passes with a heavy hammer having a slightly convex surface.

By the 19th century that process had been mechanised in London's workshops, steel rollers being used to flatten out the drawn gold wire. The occupational description gold-wire drawer most likely implied a primitive factory system in which the secondary flattening process was performed mechanically. However, it may be that the flattening process was sometimes carried out by antiquated craft techniques that may have assumed the talents of a goldbeater to finish the product.[6]

The profession of publican, which may reasonably be linked with the description inn-keeper that was applied by his descendants to Frank Hackett-Jones' grandfather, was more commonly associated with those named John Jones in early colonial New South Wales than was any trade that involved working gold. The occupation was also more in demand around Sydney town than were the skills of beating out gold leaf, or drawing gold wire. One nineteen-year-old, single, Roman Catholic John Jones from Manchester, described in the indents as a publican, was transported to Sydney in 1832 for seven years for having stolen a ring (possibly of gold?). There is no hint that he was a goldbeater by trade, and it is most unlikely that any inhabitant of Manchester in 1832 would have been. A Yorkshire John Jones of thirty-two years, also described as a publican in the indents, was sent to New South Wales for fourteen years in that same year of 1832. There is no indication that he had anything to do with the handling of gold, and Yorkshire was little better off than Lancashire as a likely haunt for gold-beaters. There is no real reason for suspecting that either of these men is relevant to our search, any more than several others of the same name from an earlier period of Sydney history who were described in convict records as a hotel-keeper or publican.

It would appear much more likely that Frank Hackett-Jones' mysterious grandfather pursued the occupation of an innkeeper in colonial New South Wales, rather than during his British existence. Interestingly, one such innkeeper named John Jones did die at Green Swamp, near Bathurst, on 5 March 1846 – that is, within two years of the birth of Charles Firman Jones at Parramatta. This man was one of two, three, or possibly four men called John Jones legally supplying cheap spirits to the thirsty inhabitants of New South Wales at some time in the years between 1843 and 1846; and his death so soon after 1844 when Charles Firman Jones was born at Parramatta might provide one good reason for a little boy being so mysteriously transferred to the care of strangers in distant Warrnambool.[7]

Of course, there were a few men named John Jones who came out to New South Wales as free and assisted migrants during the 1830s and early 1840s. A study of the *Lexigraphical Index to all Passengers to Sydney. 1828-1842* indicates approximately ten of such free men, but none had the occupation of goldbeater, or even innkeeper, against his name. Farm labourers were sought after in New South Wales at that time, and there were examples of a bricklayer, a carpenter, a tanner, and even a shoemaker named John Jones. It is very difficult to imagine why a skilled worker in gold might have been interested in an assisted passage to New South Wales at that time; or why any person in authority would have encouraged such a person to emigrate at official expense.[8]

If tracing a grandfather named John Jones in early colonial New South Wales is equivalent to pursuing the proverbial needle in a haystack, finding a grandmother named Mary Ann Firman might be thought a less daunting problem. Although the John Jones who was a worker in gold was almost certainly of convict derivation, for all we know he may have cohabited with a 'currency lass' (locally-born woman) who need not have appeared in convict records. The indexes to official New South Wales convict marriage banns for the period between 1826 and 1841 include some twenty-eight references to the name John Jones but they contain no reference to a woman with the surname Firman, either as a convict party to marriage, or as the free spouse of a convict. Neither does any female of the name Firman appear in the detailed index of ecclesiastical marriage records (compiled by the Archives Office of New South Wales) for that period. Of course, if the lady had been married in some obscure bush settlement by a transient clergyman, then the record might not have survived. The only marriage records then kept were those of the various religious denominations.

Firman was not a common surname in New South Wales, and appears very rarely in any of the several detailed muster records for that State during the period up to 1837. In the 1828 New South Wales census, one male with the surname Firsman did appear, and that was almost certainly a misprint of Firman. The name does appear regularly in later 19th-century births, deaths and marriages records; and doubtless more people of that name came out during the 1850s gold rush. It is of interest, given the naming of Rev. Charles Firman Jones in 1844, that the only Firman to be found in New South Wales marriage records for the period before 1856 was one Charles Firman who was married at Parramatta in 1844 to Mary Paterson. When Charles Firman died in 1875, his father was described in the relevant indexes as William Firman. If Mary Ann Firman was a free resident of New South Wales during the late 1830s or early 1840s, then it is possible that the Charles Firman who married at Parramatta in the exact year of Charles Firman Jones' birth was her brother or close relative, and that the naming of Rev. Charles Firman Jones perpetuated his memory. On the other hand, if the boy who was baptised Charles Jones had close relatives in New South Wales, it is harder to explain how he was brought up by foster parents in a far-distant colonial home.[9]

The two women in New South Wales records of that era with the appropriate name of Mary Ann Firman each appear unlikely contenders for the position of mother to Rev. Charles Firman Jones. On 15 September 1838, the migrant ship *Woodbridge* anchored in Port Jackson.

Numbered among its contingent was a Baptist farm labourer from Sussex named Walter Firman. His mother had been Mary Firman of Brede in Sussex. He brought with him his wife, twenty-six-year-old Mary Ann Firman, along with three young children of whom the baby daughter also carried her mother's name. There is no reason to believe that this lady would have deserted her family for a Parramatta publican, when in her mid-thirties. Of course, it is possible that she was widowed in the years after her arrival in Sydney. There is no evidence in extant marriage records of the colony to suggest that this particular Mary Ann Firman (or any other of that name) ever remarried. However, she is the only person (apart from her baby daughter) who can be positively identified as having used the name Mary Ann Firman in New South Wales at about the time when Charles Firman Jones was born. Hence this lady must be considered a possible parent for the child brought up among strangers hundreds of miles away.[10]

Convict-indent indexes that cover the period 1788 to 1842 do contain references to the Firman surname, indicating that other people of that name were present in New South Wales. There was thus no necessity for Allan Hackett-Jones to have gone back to England to search for his grandmother in the Somerset House records. A convict named Edward Firman was transported by the ship *Hebe* in 1820, and it is possible that he might have sired a daughter named Mary Ann who might have been of child-bearing age in 1844; although I found no trace of such a person in New South Wales' archival records. Another man named Edward Firman was transported on the *Hooghly* at the end of 1834, and is less likely to have fathered a 'currency lass' to fit our time schedules. However, the peculiar circumstances of Charles Firman Jones' upbringing among strangers in a distant place, and that his birthplace in 1844 was given as Parramatta, incline this author to think that his mother was probably a convict woman who had probably not entered into a marriage contract. The circumstance was a notoriously common one.

Although no person of the name Mary Ann Firman can be found in the convict-indent indexes for the period 1788 to 1842, a young lady of very similar name does appear. The only female convict in New South Wales to carry that unusual surname was one Maria Firman. She came out on the *Surrey* on 13 November 1840, as one of a cargo of 213 females who had offended against the laws of their homeland. Maria Firman was then a twenty-year-old kitchen maid with no education and no children. She hailed from Suffolk, where Allan Hackett-Jones had unsuccessfully searched for records of his grandmother. Tried at Bury St Edmunds for stealing money, Maria Firman received a sentence of seven years transportation. This was of course as good as a life sentence. Maria had no former convictions, but for a servant girl to steal money from her employers was regarded as a heinous crime. As the sentencing of women to transportation ceased in 1839, she must have been one of the last female convicts to land in New South Wales.

This young lady does not come across in the official record as an unusual beauty. Just under five feet tall, she had light brown hair and grey eyes, and a complexion described as 'ruddy and pock-pitted'. All in all, this description is a match for that of John Jones, the gold-wire drawer from London. Maria Firman arrived in the colony on 14 July 1840, and may therefore have mothered Charles Firman Jones in 1844, when still in her early twenties. Given the vagaries of names in official records at that time, and the common tendency for convict women to 'manipulate' names to avoid connections with their past, it is a small jump from Maria Firman to

Mary Ann Firman. Whether or not this be the real answer to the problem of finding Frank Hackett-Jones' paternal grandmother, that grandmother would have been some equally obscure and inconsequential inhabitant of the primitive colony of New South Wales, the great majority of whose population in 1844 was of convict derivation. Although the name Mary Ann was extremely common in lists of female convicts of that time and place, the name Maria was uncommon among British-born women.[11]

It is, therefore, an interesting coincidence that when John Jones, the keeper of the Green Man Inn near Bathurst drank himself to death in 1846, the licence to that inn was soon afterwards taken up by a woman (presumably his widow) calling herself Maria Jones. It would have made a good story: Rev. Charles Firman Jones, the son of obscure parents associated with innkeeping whose father literally drank himself to death, became a Methodist minister and spent his life in promoting the drinking of water and tea. Unfortunately that nice hypothesis will not do, and we need to look elsewhere among the New South Wales publicans named John Jones, for the real grandfather of Frank Hackett Jones. The Maria Jones of those hotel licence records was not Maria Firman of the convict indents.

Two years prior to the birth of Charles Firman Jones at Parramatta in December 1842, the *Sydney Morning Herald* recorded the marriage at Trinity Church Bathurst of John Jones Esq. of Wellington, to Maria, relict of the late A. Levingstone Esq., of Green Swamp, Bathurst. Such a lady can hardly be the Mary Ann Firman of Charles Firman Jones' Wedding Certificate, nor is she likely to be the Maria Firman who arrived in the colony as a convict spinster in the middle of 1840. Neither does it seem likely that the chap who drank himself to death within four years of marrying that eligible widow at Bathurst, was siring children in distant Parramatta. The possibility remains that Maria Firman might have been a servant at the New Inn at Green Swamp, become pregnant to the landlord, and returned to the Female Factory at Parramatta to deliver her child during 1844. However, that possibility appears remote. When Charles Jones was baptised at St John's Church in Parramatta in December 1840 his father's abode was given as Parramatta. That baptism in a respectable Anglican church argues against the baby having been the product of a liaison with an occupant of the Female Factory.[12]

Convicts needed permission to marry, and detailed records survive of those male and female convicts who were either permitted to marry, or refused permission to marry, between 1831 and 1851. The surname Firman does not occur in those convict marriage records between the year 1840, when Maria Firman arrived at Sydney, and 1851. That is, for the first decade after her arrival in New South Wales, Maria Firman does not seem to have made any attempt at legally recognised marriage. Perhaps that 'pock-marked' complexion limited her opportunities? It was a notorious fact of New South Wales life before 1838 that the women disembarking from incoming convict transports were lined up soon after arrival, and encouraged to look their best, so that the young and sexually attractive could be 'creamed off' to serve the more privileged inhabitants of the colony. Those remaining often found themselves consigned to government institutions at Parramatta.

The convict marriage entries for those named John Jones in the relevant period have been checked. Despite these entries being numerous, none married a woman with a name anything like Maria Firman, or Mary Ann Firman. The closest that one can get is the thirty-year-old John Jones who had arrived on the *Morlay 5* with a life sentence, who married a locally born sixteen-year-old girl, Mary Ann Fuller, at Pitt Town in 1840. The Christian name Mary Ann was popular at the time, and this lady is highly unlikely to relate to our Mary Ann Firman and John Jones linkage problem.

Neither is there any record of our gold and silver wire drawer from London, who had arrived on the *Georgiana* in July 1831, having attempted to marry anybody during that decade after Maria Firman's arrival. Indeed, although the Convict Marriage Bann indexes for the earlier period 1826-1841 include many men of the name John Jones, they make no reference to any such who voyaged on the ship *Georgiana*. The detailed available evidence suggests that this Londoner, already much older than the average convict on his arrival in 1831, did not enter into any formal marriage contract prior to obtaining his Certificate of Freedom in 1840. That does not carry any implication of a life of monastic celibacy, given the common practice of the colony. Most John Joneses who did enter into formal contracts married convict women, but several married younger women who had come free and single to the colonies on emigrant ships. Sometimes a John Jones would marry a local 'currency lass' who was a convict's daughter.

A John Jones was sometimes refused permission to marry the lady of his desire, usually because one or other had previously been married and could not produce proof of their spouse's death. Occasionally, the lady's credentials could not be verified, indicating that she was living under an assumed name in the colony. Thus a twenty-seven-year-old John Jones who had arrived on the *Charles Kerr* was in November 1842 refused permission to marry twenty-three-year-old Ellen McMann, on the grounds that 'no such female as Ellen McMann arrived per *Margaret* in 1837'. That particular John Jones did not suffer from the effects of a prolonged broken heart, because the marriage records indicate that he was allowed to marry the twenty-three-year-old convict, Alice McMahon, in December 1842. Ellen McMann and Alice McMahon were the same lady, who must have been aged about sixteen years when sentenced. The use of variant names was so common in New South Wales that the problem of tracing Mary Ann Firman and the right John Jones is complicated. But any convict attempting to marry would have had to satisfy authority as to his or her identity in the official record. I have found no evidence that Mary Ann (Maria?) Firman and John Jones, of Frank Hackett-Jones' ancestral tree, ever married.[13]

As for the Parramatta birthplace, westward of the main settlement at Sydney, few places could have been more suited to such an obscure and mysterious birth as that of the baby who matured to be Rev. Charles Firman Jones. The first volume of Manning Clark's *A History of Australia* vividly described the unfortunate situation of many an English girl who came to Parramatta during the first four decades of the 19th century:

> The Governor's secretary and the superintendent of convicts conducted the muster on the ship. Women with property were immediately granted tickets-of-leave, and women with husbands in the colony were assigned to them. The rest were assigned for domestic service either in Sydney or one of the settlements, or sent to work in the female factory at Parramatta which opened in 1804 on the first floor of the new gaol there. These were taken by boat from Sydney Cove to Parramatta. This journey lasted from morning till evening in fair weather, but with an adverse wind darkness came down before the end of the journey, when great irregularities took place and the women frequently arrived at Parramatta in a state of intoxication and plundered of their property, to begin their servitude the next day in destitution and on a hangover. By an odd irony this was

generally their first experience of life in a colony which had been created for their reformation as well as their punishment.[14]

Many of these women, whatever their British backgrounds, had suffered multiple indignities on the transports en route to Sydney. The captains and crews of ships on that long haul commonly regarded them as so many prostitutes (as many indeed had been) whose presence could make a boring and uncomfortable trip more interesting. The Select Committee on the State of Gaols in 1819 was told hair-raising stories of young women being stripped and publicly flogged with ship's rope, without provocation. The younger and prettier of these women had sometimes been put at the disposal of crews of accompanying naval escort ships; as an extra insult they were promised money they never received. Indeed, it was suggested that the captain of one transport had received rope and canvas from naval vessels in return for his generous supply of women. In his official report on the state of the Female Factory in 1820, J.T. Bigge suggested that this building was little more than an ill-organised and untidy brothel harbouring women who resorted to 'indiscriminate prostitution'.[15]

By 1840, when Maria Firman made the long trip to Sydney, the government had cleaned up its female ships' act somewhat. However, the unfortunate ladies could not expect to land in Sydney with much dignity remaining. Occasionally, women were known to make the best of their unchosen lot. One incident that struck terror into the hearts of British officialdom was the report that (on a female transport sailing the long passage down the Atlantic) a crew had been seduced by experienced London professionals who made up a goodly proportion of their vessel's human cargo. Both passengers and crew promptly abandoned said vessel at Rio de Janeiro.

Women who had been 'assigned' to the menial service of more respectable inhabitants of New South Wales sometimes preferred the idea of life at the Parramatta Female Factory to their uncomfortable private servitude. It was commonly accepted that women in that position were at the sexual disposal of their 'master'; and that notable parson-magistrate, Reverend Samuel Marsden of Parramatta, classified all adult unmarried women in New South Wales as 'concubines'. There were various ways of 'escaping' to the Female Factory, and many a young woman did not have to try at all. Roundly abusing the head of the house was one way to get to Parramatta, or alternatively being over-friendly to him or some male convict in the vicinity could easily result in a pregnant convict woman finding herself 'lying in' at Parramatta's Female Factory. By July 1840 when Maria Firman arrived at Sydney, although the 'assignment system' had not finally been terminated, convicts were no longer sent to new terms of assignment in colonial private households. That young lady presumably served a term within some part of the government penal system, and Parramatta was a not unlikely environment with which to make an early acquaintance.

Parramatta in the early 1840s was little different to the settlement described by the much-travelled convict-ship's surgeon P. Cunningham in his book entitled *Two Years in New South Wales*, published in London in 1827.

> The main road from Sydney runs on in a line with George Street toward Parramatta; another road strikes off to the left of this, about the sixth milestone, towards Liverpool, and thence on to the southern counties of Argyle and Westmoreland. Just before reaching Parramatta, a road turns off to join that leading to Liverpool, which town it connects with Parramatta. One road turning off from the portion of the town of Parramatta situated beyond the river, runs backward along the

right bank of the stream toward Sydney, to communicate with the numerous farms upon that line; while three others branch off toward the interior from near this point.

Convict women were not the only inhabitants of New South Wales to form the impression that 'all roads lead to Parramatta'.[16]

Cunningham described a sprawling settlement of detached cottages with their own gardens, and some superior two-storeyed dwellings 'built with great taste and elegance'. The infant Charles Firman Jones is unlikely to have been closely acquainted with such 'superior' architecture. Cunningham also noted that 'The soldiers' barrack, the convict barrack, and the jail, are all rather prominent'. He further noted an 'established church' and a 'dissenting chapel', while across the bridge about a quarter-mile away 'you come to the Female Factory, surrounded by its twelve-feet high wall, which however, some of its liberty-loving inmates occasionally find no great difficulty in clambering over'. The Scottish Governor, Thomas Brisbane, had made his main residence at Government House in Parramatta and had built an observatory there to pursue his interest in surveying the heavenly bodies.

The not-so-heavenly bodies dwelling at the Female Factory did not find Parramatta such an attractive environment as Cunningham depicted, even when it was clothed in the splendours of early spring: 'The cottages, of purest white, shining in our clear cloudless sky like transparent alabaster, gemming over the fresh green undulating carpet beneath and around you ...' Whatever her real background, 'Mary Ann Firman' was probably more aware of the dramatic seasonal transformation under 'the fervid summer heats', more especially around December of 1844 when she was about to give birth to Charles Firman Jones.

> The fields now exhibit a deadly brown lurid hue, as if life were never more to animate them; the very grass becoming so parched and crisp, that you may rub it to powder between your palms – and the bushy evergreens which clothe the rising grounds around powdered thickly with the floating dust![17]

The lives of many New South Wales convicts, of both sexes, were radically changed by a new situation emerging in the colony during the early 1840s. The time-honoured system of convicts being forced to work as assigned servants wherever and for whomsoever officialdom desired to 'assign' them, finally ceased in 1842. Large numbers of convicts were either free by having served their sentences, or worked for masters of their own choosing on tickets-of-leave. The colony's pastoral industry, which had provided the basis for development and rapid expansion of the settlement during the 1830s, crashed catastrophically in the years 1842-43. Many pastoralists, for whom ex-convicts had continued to work as shepherds after the expiry of their terms of enforced assignment, found themselves unable to pay wages.

The then novel concept of bankruptcy had to be worked into New South Wales legislation, because the traditional British debtors' prisons could not possibly have handled the great rush of colonial insolvents whose number included many of the 'free and respectable' residents of the colony. It was a good time for an ex-convict who had completed his sentence and become a free man, to look for a bush inn to run. The historical conditions of life in New South Wales, where so many inhabitants were addicted to rum or cheap spirits, meant that the life of an innkeeper was viewed as a sensible escape from the drudgery of working long hours for squatters or landowners, who might not even be able to pay decent wages.

Each year in about May, *The Sydney Gazette* published long lists of publicans whose applications for liquor licences in Sydney had either been accepted or rejected by officialdom. Every city street appears to have had numerous candidates jostling for this popular colonial trade. In 1841 there were 191 applications for Sydney alone, and of 139 of those 'adjudicated upon', 50 were refused licences. Of twenty-nine new applications, only four were granted in that year. Twenty-seven previously practising Sydney publicans lost their licences that same year, when officialdom appears to have been tightening up the rules on Sydney public houses. It was noted that many had lost their licences because they offered inadequate accommodation facilities, and it was expected that licences would be renewed in cases where the innkeeper moved to more suitable premises. John Jones, who allegedly became a Parramatta innkeeper soon thereafter, was moving into a highly competitive field.[13]

Even out at Parramatta the licensing justices were deluged with applications during the early 1840s. On 19 April 1842 a Court of Petty Sessions was held at the Parramatta Court House to consider a long list of applications. There was as yet no Jones among these Parramatta candidates, the White Horse Hotel in Macquarie Street (with which a John Jones would be associated in 1844) being then run by one Edward Lakeman. There were 55 applications for liquor licenses in the immediate vicinity of Parramatta in 1842, although some applicants were disappointed. John Jones must have been fortunate to squeeze his way into that select Parramatta company during 1844.[19]

Official records of liquor licences taken out in New South Wales during the period May 1842 to February 1843 contain no references to the name John Jones, although a Samuel Jones and a Thomas Jones were involved in that thriving trade. Records for the period May 1843 to February 1844 contain references to two innkeepers of the name John Jones. One such man had recently opened the New Inn at Green Swamp on the Bathurst Road, the licence being signed at Bathurst and applicable from 1 July 1843 to 30 June 1844. The other innkeeper of that name briefly operated at Jervis Bay, and his licence signed by Illawarra magistrates applied from 14 September 1843 to 30 June 1844. There is no reference to a licence for any John Jones at Green Swamp, nor at Jervis Bay, for the period immediately after June 1844. The next extant licence for the New Inn at Green Swamp, in the name of John Jones, was signed at Bathurst on 15 April 1845, and related to the period April 1845 to March 1846. However, it does appear that the John Jones who resided near Bathurst stayed in that vicinity throughout the period July 1843 to March 1846, at which time he drank himself to death.

Another (for our purposes more interesting) John Jones of that period held the liquor licence for the White Horse Hotel at Parramatta. That licence was dated at Parramatta on the 16 April 1844, and it applied for the period May 1844 to March 1845, during which period Charles Firman Jones was born at Parramatta. If our Maria Firman of the convict indents produced a child during those years, who more likely to have fathered it than an obscure Parramatta publican who quickly disappeared from the liquor licence records? There is no record of John Jones of the White Horse Hotel in Parramatta during the next licensing period, although there is a reference to a John Jones (probably the same man) holding the licence for a quite different hotel in Parramatta. He was the licensee of the Emu Hotel in Church Street for the period April 1845 to March 1846. Thereafter, this John Jones dropped out of the liquor-licence records, and the name John Jones disappeared from the records with him.

There is no way of knowing whether the holder (or holders) of these Parramatta liquor licences around the time of Charles Firman Jones' birth had a British background in goldbeating, or in gold-wire drawing. There is no way of establishing whether he was the same John Jones who had recently held a publican's licence at Jervis Bay, near to where our convict gold wire drawer had operated during the later 1830s. Not one John Jones appeared in the indexes of records of New South Wales hotel licensees for the period April 1846 to April 1847 or in the years immediately following, when the name of Maria Jones regularly appeared as licensee of the New Inn at Green Swamp.

That strange multiplicity of hotel licences in the name of John Jones for a brief period around 1844 when Charles Firman Jones was born, contrasting as it does with the lack of such references for earlier and later periods, suggests that apart from the tippling gentleman at the New Inn (alias the Green Man) near Bathurst, one individual named 'John Jones' was responsible for three different hotel licences relating to Jervis Bay and Parramatta. Those three licences did not overlap in their periods of application, and when put together they form a fascinating jigsaw. We do not know in which year the young Charles Firman Jones was taken from Parramatta to distant Warrnambool, but it seems to have been when he was so young that he retained no memories of parents. He never spoke of them to his own children.[20]

We do know that the Parramatta Female Factory still flourished in the early and mid-1840s. As the standard reference work on that institution states:

> It was still the practice in 1841 to return all assigned pregnant female servants to the Factory Hospital when they were near the time for giving birth; and they remained at the hospital while nursing their children.

The assignment system ceased to function during 1842, and after December 1842 the number of women and children in residence began gradually to decline. However on 1 January 1845, soon after Charles Firman Jones was born somewhere in Parramatta in obscure circumstances, there were still 370 women and 123 children in residence at the Parramatta Female Factory. The fact that Charles Jones, the son of a Parramatta innkeeper, was baptised in St. John's Church of England in Parramatta late in 1844 might suggest that his mother was not then a regular inhabitant of the Female Factory. However, it is likely that the baby was born at the Factory's infirmary, which was generally used by district women at the time of 'confinement'.[21]

The Hacketts

Frank Hackett-Jones' mother (second wife of Rev. Charles Firman Jones) was Lizzie Jane Hackett, born in Melbourne during the hectic days of the Victorian alluvial gold rushes on 11 September 1856. The gold rushes of the 1850s attracted a mix of enterprising free immigrants from around the world, and would transform the earlier colonial population largely derived from a convict background. Lizzie Jane's Irish-gentleman father James Hackett had not long arrived in the new colony of Victoria, where convict ships had not appeared for several years.

James Hackett had been born in King's County, Ireland, in 1823, and would marry four times. He first married a cousin, Eliza Jones, at Horseleap in Ireland's County Westmeath on 27 January 1851. His first child, Henry W. Hackett was born at Tyrellspass in Westmeath in February 1852. A daughter, who lived only a few months, was born at Melbourne on 3 March 1854, which suggests that the family had emigrated during 1852-53. Family tradition has it that James Hackett's first bride suffered from tuberculosis, and that the family emigrated to a sunnier climate for her sake. Melbourne's climate proved of little avail, and Eliza Hackett died at the age of twenty-three years on 17 March 1855. She was buried in the Wesleyan section of the newly opened Melbourne General Cemetery at Carlton.

James Hackett apparently enjoyed the married state, because within nine months of his first bride's death he remarried. Lizzie Jane Hackett (mother of Frank Hackett-Jones) was the eldest of four children of James Hackett's second marriage, of whom only two survived infancy. Her mother, Mary Ann Thompson, hailed from Queen's County in Ireland, and had immigrated to Hobart with her sister Ellen in 1853. Like thousands of her countrywomen she fled a land stricken by the aftermath of the Irish potato famine of the 1840s. Married at the 'Wesleyan Home Cottage' by Rev. D. J. Draper on the 11 December 1855, Mary Ann Hackett's married life was to be short. Aged twenty-five years at her marriage, she died at about the same time as her fourth son, Joseph, who died aged five months in May 1862. Lizzie Jane was only about seven years of age when her father, James Hackett, married Caroline Bolton, near the end of 1863.

James Hackett, second son of a member of the lesser Irish gentry, probably had little to expect at home, so he sought opportunities for advancement in a new land far-famed for its rich gold deposits. Men from a respectable and educated background were few, and likely to obtain official positions. On arrival in Melbourne James Hackett was described in official documents as a farmer, but he soon became a public servant connected with the administration of what we know as the Old Melbourne Gaol in Swanston Street. This branch of the Melbourne Hacketts thus appears to have been connected with the oversight of locally convicted persons, rather than of men transported for crimes in England. Many prisoners at the jail were doubtless of British or Irish convict background or descent. His address at the time of his second wife's death was given as the Officers' Quarters at the Melbourne Gaol in Swanston Street, and Mary Ann Hackett apparently died there in 1862.[22]

During that hectic gold rush era, Melbourne felt an acute need for jails and jailers. George Wintle, Melbourne's first jail governor, had at that time three different city prisons under his supervision. The building with which James Hackett was associated was that known to later generations as 'the Old Melbourne Gaol'. It is today preserved as a fascinating if somewhat macabre museum, forever associated in the popular mind with the hanging of the notorious bushranger Ned Kelly. The decision to build this 'new prison' was made at Sydney in 1841, and inhabitants of the Port Phillip District were initially suspicious of the motives of 'big

Mary Ann Thompson, mother of Lizzie Jane Hackett

brother' at Sydney: 'it looked so like a fortress built to overawe the straggling township below, or to imprison its inhabitants if they should prove refractory to the authorities in Sydney ...' Opened on the first day of January in 1845, the new jail then housed 59 male and nine female prisoners.

A treadmill was soon thereafter added to the prison's 'standard furnishings', but as it required fifteen high-stepping prisoners to keep this machine in motion it served little purpose until the goldfields provided a more ready supply of sturdy villains during the 1850s. At that time 'between the years 1851 and 1860, ... the scoundrelism of New South Wales and Van Diemen's Land, and even of San Francisco, poured into Melbourne, and had to be repressed by such inadequate means as were then available'. Presumably James Hackett was pleased to see the clumsy treadmill being used for those purposes of 'repression' for which it had been ingeniously designed by local backers of law and order.[23]

The jail property at the junction of La Trobe and Swanston Streets (on the edge of the City of Melbourne) still covered more than ten acres in the early 1860s when James Hackett lived there.[24] Family tradition has it that Hackett was governor of the Old Melbourne Gaol, but a close scrutiny of *Victorian Government Gazettes* for that period provides no support for that idea. He was most likely a lesser officer on the staff of that jail, his occupation being given on marriage certificates and like documents as civil servant. The fact that in 1862 James Hackett apparently lived with his wife on the jail premises indicates that his role involved close associations with prisoners.

It is not difficult to understand why Frank Hackett-Jones would always show a keen interest in his Hackett lineage. Sir Walter Hackett had been a knight of King Edward I in the County of Nottingham. Exactly when the Hackett family established itself in Ireland is unclear, but there are references to a family named Haket in Tipperary during the late 13th century, and the surname appears to be of Norman origins. Edward McLysaght claimed that the family came to Ireland with the Anglo-Norman invasions of the later 12th century. Sir John Hackett became Henry VIII's ambassador at Ulster in the 16th century. Sir Thomas Hackett, a Lord Mayor of Dublin late in the 17th century, is described in *Burke's General Armory* as 'descended from an ancient family, long settled in Ireland'. Among the Irish Hacketts treated in *Burke's General Armory* there is a Hackett of Hackettstown, in County Carlow. Many eminent Irish Hacketts belonged to the Roman Catholic faith, but ancestors of James Hackett were linked to the Church of Ireland's (Anglican) flock. James appears to have early come under Methodist influence in Ireland, and a Methodist celebrated his Melbourne marriage to Mary Ann Thompson in 1855. James Hackett allegedly loaned money for the construction of Melbourne's Wesley Church, where he was a regular attender.[25]

Several branches of this long-established Irish family contributed significant sons to Australian society. Charles Prendergast Hackett of Trinity College, Dublin, was admitted to the Irish Bar in 1842, and came to Melbourne via India in 1854. In time, he became a prominent member of Victoria's County Court judiciary. John Winthrop Hackett was another from Trinity College, Dublin, admitted to the Irish Bar in 1874. He came to Melbourne in 1876, to the position of Vice-Principal of Trinity College in the University of Melbourne. By 1882 he was in Western Australia, where he became a prominent newspaper proprietor and sometime political colleague of Sir John Forrest. His son, General Sir John

Hackett, would achieve fame as Commander in Chief of the British Army on the Rhine, and afterwards as Principal of King's College in the University of London.[26]

James Hackett, the 'farmer' and jail official in Melbourne, appears to have been a poor relation to those eminent colonial Hacketts. An article on his son J.T. Hackett describes the father as hailing from Broughal Castle, Frankford (now Kilcormack) in King's County. The family's Melbourne domestic context was less impressive. James Hackett's third wife, Caroline Bolton, did not long survive the others. She bore two children, Fossey Bolton (25 June 1865) and Caroline Matilda Gibbons (28 April 1870), herself dying near the end of the year 1870. At that date Lizzie Jane Hackett was fourteen years old, and henceforth she would take much of the responsibility for looking after her own younger brother James, and Caroline Bolton's two small motherless children. James Hackett Sr urgently needed another wife to look after his young brood, and by September 1871 he had married Emma Gluyas Pascoe. His family did not consider that his choice of wives improved with advancing years, and Emma Pascoe has come down in family tradition as 'an unscrupulous woman' who made her stepchildren's lives a misery by exploiting her own children (born in 1873 and 1877) as domestic spies.[27]

In that unhappy situation, Lizzie Jane Hackett stayed on as defender of the children of Hackett's earlier marriages against an allegedly heartless stepmother. Fossey Bolton, born at Melbourne in June 1865, would become an artist and a poet. He was sent to prison on the initiative of his own father, James Hackett, for threatening his cruel stepmother. Lizzie Hackett, despite her amiable nature, never forgave her father for what she considered a cruel injustice to her victimised younger half-brother. Her main escape from that nasty domestic situation was to holiday with her mother's Irish sister, by then married to a Hobart man named Kennedy. She was always welcome to stay with the Kennedy family, and Lizzie enjoyed the very different domestic environment at Hobart. Growing up with early responsibilities in that difficult and emotionally demanding situation, Lizzie Jane Hackett developed into a capable and affectionate woman with a deep concern for other people and their problems. When the Methodist Minister Charles Firman Jones was himself left a widower in 1890, Lizzie Jane Hackett (by then in her mid-thirties) would have made an ideal minister's wife.

Her unfortunate younger half-brother, Fossey Bolton Hackett, died on 21 October 1891 in Hawthorn at the age of twenty-six, apparently of tuberculosis and asthma. His death certificate indicated that the young lithographic artist had travelled widely through South Australia, Queensland and New South Wales. His young widow, named

Lizzie Jane Hackett

Drawing by Fossey Bolton Hackett, found in the waste paper basket by Frank's mother, Lizzie Jane Hackett (Fossey's half-sister).

Hannah Stanley Oughton at the time of her marriage, would remarry and know better times as the wife of a politician in Western Australia.

Joneses and Hacketts

Charles Firman Jones, father of Frank Hackett-Jones and husband of Lizzie Jane Hackett, had been educated from an early age by god-fearing people near Warrnambool on Victoria's rural south west coast, and far from his Parramatta birthplace. How he came to Warrnambool is unclear, but he obviously learned to reject that innkeeping family background from an early age. In his early twenties he was deeply moved by a religious revival movement, and decided to train for the ministry of the Wesleyan Church in Victoria. His first ministerial appointment in 1868 was at Seymour on the Melbourne-Sydney Road. Seymour was situated inland from Australia's Great Dividing Range in a largely pastoral setting, and when Charles Jones moved on in 1870 it was to a Methodist charge at Deniliquin, further north-east and across the Murray River in New South Wales. Having arrived back in the State of his birth in 1870, Charles Firman Jones would spend the remainder of his long life there.

While he had been the Wesleyan minister at Deniliquin, Charles Jones came to know Elizabeth Emily Louise Jones. She was a daughter of David Griffith Jones, proprietor and editor of *The Pastoral Times*, which was published at Deniliquin. By 1872 Rev. Charles Firman Jones had moved on to Queanbeyan (near the site of modern Canberra) and in 1874 he was Wesleyan minister at inland Crookwell, further north-west on a tributary of the Lachlan River. At that point he married Elizabeth Emily Jones whom he had met while at Deniliquin, and in 1877 he returned to the Methodist charge of Deniliquin where his father-in-law had died in December 1876. Rev. Charles Firman Jones probably assisted his mother-in-law with editing *The Pastoral Times*, before officially taking over as manager-editor after her death.

The death certificate of the widow of the founding proprietor, dated 26 January 1880, described her as 'proprietress of newspaper'. Described in her own journal (probably by the incoming editor, Rev. Charles Firman Jones) as 'of a kindly and benevolent disposition', the lady died of pneumonia after a brief illness. Rev. Charles Jones then took leave of absence from church duties to become editor-manager of *The Pastoral Times* during 1880 and 1881. The official *Australasian Methodist Ministerial General Index* described the Rev. Charles Jones' state at that time as one of 'resting'. That Methodist minister with no personal background in the pastoral industry possibly found his new role demanding, although he would always enjoy discussing agricultural matters with men on the land. His earliest years lived amidst the fertile volcanic soils of Victoria's Warrnambool district had probably given him some agricultural experience.[28]

In 1880 the Deniliquin district was a flourishing pastoral area, directly linked to Melbourne rather than to Sydney by a railway that crossed the Murray River (and its Customs Office) into Victoria at Echuca:

> The district pastures more than a million sheep and ten thousand horses and cattle; the pure-bred herds and flocks, of which there are several, attract many customers; agriculture is increasing every year, and already some of the large freehold estates are being divided so that they may be leased or sold for farming purposes.

Deniliquin's Pastoral Society was noted for the excellence of its sheep shows. There was obviously a lot happening in 1880s Riverina for the editor of *The Pastoral Times* to observe and write about.[29]

Editorials in *The Pastoral Times* during the period when Rev. Charles Firman Jones was manager-editor tended to be lengthy, and trenchant in their opinions. They contained many hallmarks of that worthy minister's Sabbath-day sermons, but their subject matter was more often colonial politics and economics than spiritual matters. Frank Hackett-Jones' father held strong free trade views, at a time when the major political groupings in the Australian colonies were designated either protectionist or free trade. Rev. Charles Jones indicated those same suspicions of 'working class ignorance' that his son would much later express while living in retirement at Adelaide. The colony of Victoria, with which the New South Wales Riverina town of Deniliquin had close trading links, was then the home of official policies of economic 'protection' via tariffs on imported goods, and of controlled immigration to protect living conditions of its colonial labour force. At a time when a radical Victorian Government headed by the Melbourne suburban shopkeeper Graeme Berry appeared to threaten the security of large landholders, Rev. Charles Jones' Deniliquin editorials blasted 'scheming politicians' and 'grasping master tradesmen'. His fiery editorials doubtless helped sell many papers to colonial landholders.

Frank Hackett-Jones' father was extremely industrious. While fulminating through the editorial columns of *The Pastoral Times* on matters political, economic and miscellaneous, he continued his connection with the local Methodist pulpit for some time. Periodic notices in *The Pastoral Times* under the heading of 'Wesley Church' advertised his Sabbath-day activities: 'The Rev. Charles Jones will conduct Divine Service on Sabbath next, at Harbourne 11 a.m., Wesley Chase at 2:30 p.m., and at Deniliquin in the evening'. Ordinary followers of John Wesley might enjoy a leisurely Sabbath day; but not those who carried on his tradition of energetic horseback preaching itineraries. Occasionally, the conclusion

Charles Firman Jones

Charles Jones, the Methodist parson prepares for duty.

to a fiery political editorial might end with a note from the Methodist pulpit. Thus, after blasting ignorant workers and 'scheming politicians' of Melbourne, Rev. Charles Jones ended a thundering 'Free Trade' editorial on an ominous note: 'verily it were better for the pitiful grasping hypocrites that a millstone were hanged about their neck and they were cast into the sea'. Something of this tendency not to suffer fools gladly always remained with his son, Frank Hackett-Jones.[30]

The columns of *The Pastoral Times* were occasionally used for characteristically Methodist purposes in those years of the early 1880s. When in 1881 a meeting of local churchmen and other interested persons could not agree on whether to form a total abstinence society, or the softer option of a temperance society, the Deniliquin periodical's columns swung forcibly into the argument. The reverend editor was very clear that any society that aimed at curbing alcoholic abuses had to be built on a 'total abstinence' basis. He contended that some men who were 'moderate' drinkers most of the time became helpless victims on rare occasions of celebration, and needed 'total' protection from tempting liquid concoctions of a thirsty Australian inland. Almost a century later, that minister-editor's ageing son, Frank Hackett-Jones, would retain equally strong feelings against the use of alcohol at Methodist functions.[31]

On 30 March 1880, Rev. Charles Jones had been entertained at a 'Complimentary Tea Meeting' by the public of Deniliquin, on the occasion of his giving up the pulpit of Wesley Church to become a full-time journal editor. It was almost a decade since he had come to Deniliquin, as the town's first regularly appointed Wesleyan minister, and during his ministry there a church building had been erected and almost paid off. Deniliquin's mayor, Dr J.P. Noyes, chaired the festivities while 400 locals enjoyed 'vocal and instrumental music' supplied in Rev. Charles Jones' honour.[32]

Whether or not he enjoyed 'resting' from pulpit duties, by 1882 Rev. Charles Jones was back and active in the Methodist ministry, preaching at the small gold settlement of Adelong (in the hill country south of Gundagai) between 1882 and 1884. From 1885 to 1887, he was the Methodist minister at the small south-eastern New South Wales coastal settlement of Shoalhaven, near the mouth of the river of the same name. By 1888 Rev. Charles Jones had made sufficient impression upon the local Methodist scene to be invited to become the minister of Sydney's Wesley Church, where he was serving his Church when his first wife (Elizabeth Emily, née Jones), died in March 1890. It is unclear how Lizzie Jane Hackett met the Sydney Methodist minister, but presumably she was then visiting Sydney. On 8 September 1891, she became the second wife of Rev. Charles Firman Jones.

The marriage took place at the Hackett family home in the Melbourne suburb of Carlton, and the marriage certificate gave Melbourne as the bride's normal place of abode. At the age of thirty-five years, the diminutive Lizzie Jane Hackett was taking on a daunting role. Her Methodist minister husband had three surviving children from his first marriage to Elizabeth Emily Jones, four children of that union having died in infancy. Lizzie Jane was long accustomed to caring for motherless children within her own childhood domestic environment, but the wife of a Methodist minister was also expected to play a useful role in congregational life.

Having married a Methodist minister of the great metropolis, Lizzie Jane Jones (née Hackett) would follow him further and further from the heart of things. From 1891 to 1893 the Jones family lived in the parsonage at Rockdale adjacent to Botany Bay, and then part of Sydney's remoter southern outskirts. It was there that Lizzie Jane brought Frank Harold Jones into the world, on 9 July 1892. The area around Rockdale had been slow to develop, but a Wesleyan Church had been built there as early as 1858, as one of the district's first symbols of European civilisation. Little changed around Rockdale until, with great pomp and ceremony, the Redfern to Hurstville section of the Illawarra railway was opened late in 1884. Rockdale was then treated to the very unusual presence of a special train loaded with dignitaries, including several cabinet ministers. As with most people who came to the village of Rockdale, those distinguished citizens were merely 'passing through', bound for a splendid official luncheon at a resort centre that appropriately overlooked Botany Bay. During those years of the late 19th century, Rockdale municipality was developed as a seaside resort area for city folk.

Having Rockdale for a birthplace might not be considered any great advantage in life. On the other hand, Frank Jones would probably not have preferred the alternative description of his place of origins, 'at Botany Bay'. Whatever imagery the name Rockdale might summon before the reader's mind, throughout the Anglo-Saxon world Botany Bay has long had its own peculiar associations. As an official history of the municipality of Rockdale proudly pointed out, the municipality was closely associated with the very earliest planning for European settlement in 'the great south land'. The environs of Botany Bay so impressed those eminent eighteenth-century British visitors Captain James Cook and Sir Joseph Banks that this obscure stretch of swamp-bound water was chosen as the first site for permanent British settlement in 'New Holland'. European visitors to the great southern continent have seldom been good judges of what they thought they saw. Hence, when Captain Arthur Phillip duly arrived at Botany Bay in 1788, with his cargo of convicted felons exported 'for their country's good', he was not impressed by those green meadows of which Joseph Banks had spoken. In fact, those meadows were reed-encrusted tidal swamplands, but (as with much Australian swampland) when summer came there would be precious little fresh water to support a settlement.

Although Botany Bay was hastily abandoned to its Aboriginal occupants (being mainly used as a source of seashells in order to create mortar lime for the new settlement of Sydney), its original fame was not extinguished. The dubious merits of Botany Bay continued to provide a theme for songs and ballads lustily intoned in the narrow laneways of London and in England's industrial cities, whence many of the earliest involuntary settlers of New South Wales came. English Gypsies, of whom not a few would end up as convict bullock drivers flogging and cursing their beasts under the sweltering summer skies of the great Australian interior, had their own name for Botany Bay: *bitcheno padlengresky tem* or 'transported fellow's country'. To what extent the elderly Frank Hackett-Jones valued the historical significance of his place of origin, or even thought about it, this author is unclear. I never heard him mention it.[33]

Baby Frank was less than two years of age when the Methodist Conference moved his father to the charge of West Maitland (well to Sydney's north, in the Newcastle area) where he would minister from 1894 to 1897. It was at West Maitland that Frank Jones' only brother, Allan, was born on 5 July 1896. Frank Harold Jones spent his preschool years at West Maitland, but it is not surprising that in his old age he remembered little from that period. A large St Bernard dog made sufficient imprint on the boy's memory to be long remembered, as did those pleasant 'maiden neighbours', the Misses Quiggen. His memoirs made virtually no reference to the presence of the older children of Rev. Charles Jones, his half-brothers and half-sister, but their needs, in conjunction with the demands of a Methodist parsonage, must have largely detracted from the attention paid by Lizzie Jane to her new baby.

About a decade before Frank Jones came with his parents to West Maitland, the town was vividly written up (complete with lithograph illustrations of the township, of its main street, and of the Anglican church) in *The Picturesque Atlas of Australasia*. Maitland was divided by a substantial stream known as Wallis' Creek:

> East Maitland, laid out on high and dry ground, is the Government town; but West Maitland, laid out on the alluvial flat by the riverside as a private town, took the public fancy more; and though occasionally liable to floods, has become the principal place of business.

The rich alluvial soil was indeed very flood prone, and West Maitland's main street and business centre required extensive engineering works to prevent it being washed into the floods.[34]

That lithograph of West Maitland township in the later 1880s shows several church towers and steeples standing starkly against the skyline. It was a comfortable setting for a minister of the Church: 'the churches make display of faith by solid and beautiful works'. The author who thus wrote up West Maitland for *The Picturesque Atlas* thought that the environment adversely affected its inhabitants: 'there is an indolent air about everything and everybody – an air of contentment and confidence. The richness of the soil seems to impart an infection of trustful laziness'. We can be confident that Rev. Charles Firman Jones discouraged such symptoms in his own family and in his parishioners, although doubtless he enjoyed discussing agricultural matters with local farmers who tilled productive soil. A laconic and often silent man when not in the pulpit, he was at his most conversational with farming folk after church.

In 1897, the Methodist Conference called Rev. Charles Firman Jones to be minister at Wagga Wagga, which meant returning to that Riverina District in which he had spent many years during an earlier phase of his ministry and during his period as manager-editor of *The Pastoral Times*. Between 1897 and 1900 the infant Frank Harold Jones would begin his formal kindergarten education at Wagga Wagga.

CHAPTER 2

GROWING UP: 1897 TO 1909

The aged Frank Hackett-Jones' earliest clear memories were of life with his parents at the Methodist parsonage at Wagga Wagga, between 1897 and 1900. At that time Wagga Wagga was no longer an important Murrumbidgee River port for paddle steamers towing barges of wool, having been linked to both Melbourne and Sydney by railway well before 1900. The district was largely pastoral, although smaller farm-holdings were far more numerous than in earlier decades.

Even at the end of the 19th century, Wagga Wagga retained ('enjoyed' might be the wrong word) some international fame thanks to a local butcher of the late 1860s. Thomas Castro's attempts to pass himself off as the true heir to the rich English Tichborne inheritance led to his conviction of perjury, and earned him many years in an English jail.

Deniliquin had been the home of that respectable journal for graziers, *The Pastoral Times*, managed and edited for a time by Rev. Charles Firman Jones.

Frank Jones' parents

However, Wagga Wagga in the 1890s was the home of *The Hummer*, the official organ of the Associated Riverina Workers and propagator of the doctrine of socialism as 'mateship'. Rev. Charles Firman Jones would not have been interested in obtaining editorial or managerial employment with that radical voice of the ignorant multitude. Frank Jones attended a private kindergarten at Wagga Wagga, and never forgot being temporarily blinded by an attack of sandy blight during the acute drought of the later 1890s. He also vividly remembered visits to the farm of the Lyons family, some seven miles from the town, 'out in the scrub'. Never a person to find public displays of emotion enjoyable, little Frank was subjected to the excruciating ordeal of having to play 'kiss in the ring' with the Lyons girls. Going out on shooting trips with

his father was less embarrassing, although Frank long retained memories of an 'alarming plank bridge' (possibly over the Murrumbidgee River) that he had to traverse on such expeditions.[1]

Primary Schooling at Orange and Kiama

From Wagga Wagga, the Jones family was called to the Methodist parsonage at Orange, many miles to the north and with a colder high-country winter climate. Frank spent his earlier primary school years there between 1900 and 1903, and would be eleven years of age when he left the district.

Frank Jones

Orange had moved off to a heady start when E.H. Hargraves made the nearby mineral discoveries that started Australia's gold rushes of the 1850s. With the rapid disappearance of that alluvial gold, life became much quieter until a railway was constructed to link the settlement with Bathurst, and Orange thereafter became an agricultural centre and a trucking depot for livestock pushed eastwards from the arid continent's sprawling interior by hardy drovers. The district scenery contrasted markedly with the dusty drought-stricken Murrumbidgee plains around Wagga Wagga, with which young Frank Jones had recently been acquainted. Orange had a comforting English look:

> The daphnes, magnolias, and oleanders of the Sydney gardens are absent, but the hawthorne hedges are vigorous, currants and gooseberries come to perfection, and the wheat harvest is later than that of Bathurst.[2]

The rich, red volcanic soil encouraged intensive agriculture, and there were grassy hills surrounding the town, behind which towered the Canoblas – peaks that remained shrouded in snow for several months of the year. Orange did not have the 'typically inland Australian' river and plain environment of Wagga Wagga, but it was another significant New South Wales rural inland centre which left a clear imprint on the mind of young Frank Jones.

Frank especially remembered the large corner block, covering a whole acre, on which the family residence sat. He learned to climb in a row of pine trees nearby, and played at marbles and spinning tops with his boyhood friend, Ray Martin. Already life had its more serious domestic responsibilities: his job was cleaning the fowl houses, to provide rich fertiliser for the parsonage gardens. His father always maintained a useful vegetable garden. He also remembered that going to school was very cold in winter, with snow piled up high against the fences. This had its enjoyable side for a little boy recently arrived from the hot and dusty plains of the

Riverina. At Orange he first learned the joys of throwing snowballs with other school children, and the building of snowmen proved a novel leisure-time activity.

At Orange's public school young Frank Jones had his first taste of homework. Going to and from school was not always an enjoyable experience for a son of the local Methodist minister. The Methodists had a reputation for being wowsers, and not all country townspeople befriended their values. Larrikins would harass young Frank on his way to and from school, and he was extremely self-conscious when passing the motley collection of local drunks, sitting aimlessly by the kerbsides disposing of cheap whisky. At Orange, little Frank himself learned how it felt to be caught out as a sinner by his somewhat fearsome father. He first experienced the shame and pain resulting from being 'dobbed in' when he was accused of smok-

Frank Jones with friend

ing by his older half-sister, who had a sensitive nose for tobacco smoke. Having bought the cigarettes by accident (apparently in a misunderstanding with a shopkeeper) little Frank decided to try them. A Methodist parsonage of that era was a bad place to indulge in such juvenile experimentation.

If the Methodist Conference had been selecting its triennial change of ministerial scenery for Rev. Charles Jones on the basis of providing an education in New South Wales geography for his children, it could hardly have done better. Having experienced the dusty river plains of Wagga Wagga in the 1890s droughts, and made snowmen in the high-country winters of Orange a little later, the growing primary-school boy Frank Jones found himself going to school at Kiama between 1903 and 1906. The Kiama district was even then a favoured part of south-eastern New South Wales' coastline:

> The peaceful village known as Jamberoo rests snugly in a valley on the right, and in front, about four score miles from Sydney, is the coast's famed gem, Kiama, noted for its beauty, its bluestone, and its blowhole.[3]

Young Frank Jones would be into his fifteenth year, and entering puberty, before he left Kiama with his family. In later years he maintained that the effects of the hell-fire preaching and the rugged conversion tactics of the Methodist minister then based at Jamberoo afflicted his personality for life, by leaving him with a false sense of guilt that he could never fully throw off.

Kiama, like Wagga Wagga and Orange, was a centre with rich soil, upon which a strong and healthy agricultural industry flourished: 'A block of forty acres here is worth more to the farmer than a square mile of ordinary country, and a railway runs almost on its boundary'. Like Orange, Kiama was set in countryside that had known intense volcanic activity in ancient times, and its basaltic bluffs overhanging the Pacific Ocean could provide spectacular viewing. Frank Jones always remembered the jumbled bluestone of the area, and the township owed some of its prosperity to the fact that much of the bluestone used in Sydney's city street construction had been shipped from district quarries through the little port of Kiama. There were also untapped coal seams in the hills nearby. Kiama might have been a more significant trading centre in that era had not its tiny port been regarded as dangerously exposed to shipping damage, especially when Pacific gales raged in from the east. Kiama remained the centre of a flourishing dairy industry, feeding two local butter factories. A picturesque old coach road still wound past the Wingecarribee Swamp, up to Moss Vale in the nearby mountains. Several decades later, Frank Jones would marry a woman who had also been brought up on the farm lands of this south-eastern coastal area of New South Wales.

In his old age Frank Hackett-Jones vividly remembered that stone-walled basalt country with its fertile paddocks, ideal for hares but unsuited to the burrowing habits of the rabbit plagues that afflicted other agricultural districts in those years. Some of his most important formative years were spent there, living in a large and impressive two-storey house on a prominent hill overlooking the little township and port. The town baths, situated one-and-a-half miles from his hilltop home, provided a favourite attraction. He never forgot the sensations associated with nearly drowning in that pool, and being rescued by a fully clothed 'big boy' who jumped in after him. It was not always easy for a clergyman's son to make close friendships in a small town, but during the latter part of his stay at Kiama young Frank would enjoy regular walks and swims with a son of the local Presbyterian minister. His associations with the families of Kiama's sparse professional families were not always so pleasant, and in old age he recalled various punch-ups with sons of a local doctor and of a district solicitor.

The newly formed Commonwealth Government strongly encouraged cadet training for all young Australians in those early years of the 20th century. In his cadet photo Frank Jones was the smallest boy of his group; among many bigger boys resplendent in their uniforms of navy blue with contrasting white haversack and stiff cap. It sounds a trifle Napoleonic now, and that rig-out must have been difficult to maintain under camp conditions. Little boys drilled conscientiously with their clumsy Westley Richards rifles, each weighing nearly seven pounds. Out on the rifle range Frank was severely disadvantaged by myopic vision, and he already wore glasses. This did not prevent him spending his pocket money on the *Boys' Own Annual*, a bound copy of which cost the huge sum of six shillings. He also bought and read the little penny paper known as *World's News*, which forecast the imminence of World War I. Young Frank Jones was already conscious of defects in the arches of his feet that made it difficult to walk without shoes, and prevented him from running and jumping effectively. He became attracted to a sport that did not require much running or jumping, and one that would remain a major interest of his adult working years: golf. At Kiama he played golf with the caddies, using 'cheap' clubs costing four shillings and sixpence, with the gutta-percha balls of that era.

His 'farmer' father very much appreciated the parsonage's large area of fertile soil for gardening, and grew the necessary cereal crops to feed the horses that dutifully carried him around his sprawling parish. That was a major reason why parsonages of that era needed to be set on extensive blocks of fertile soil. Young Frank enjoyed visits to the local blacksmith's smithy, with his father's horses that needed to be re-shod with curved protective iron plates. The smithy was a favourite social centre for old men of the town, who sat around and gossiped while the blacksmith heaved on the big bellows that made his charcoal fire white-hot, and sparks flew from his anvil as cold steel smote white-hot iron. The newly shaped and still red-hot horse-shoes would hiss loudly and emit clouds of steam when dropped into an ever-handy tub of water to cool. Back at the parsonage stables, young Frank toiled at cleaning and softening the tangled and sweaty leather harness, and sometimes had the task of moving horses to and from paddocks further out as they were rested from their labours, or when refreshed beasts were brought back into work again.

Less pleasant than his memories of old men gossiping around the town smithy was the remembrance of the Rev. Joseph Tarn, an earnest Methodist minister at the nearby village of Jamberoo. He gave monthly Sunday school addresses to the Kiama boys. A 'penitent form' took pride of place, and the assembled little sinners were strongly urged to seek their salvation from the wrath to come. Although the aged Frank Hackett-Jones could not remember any boy ever having accepted this earnest invitation to be publicly 'saved', he would always doubt whether he had fully recovered from those unnerving experiences that had so seared a sensitive and conscientious little son of the parsonage.

Young Frank Jones was undergoing a process of rapid mental as well as physical development during his Kiama phase. At the local public school he outstretched his tiny rural class, and, left to his own study resources Frank easily became dux of the primary school. This academic success in such a small pond roused him to greater ambitions, and at fourteen years of age he sat the examinations required to obtain a scholarship to Sydney Boys' High School, at that time one of only two State boys' high schools in New South Wales. Evidently, he missed out on that scholarship, which would have meant a lot to his fond parents. But he would briefly attend Sydney Boys' High School right at the end of his period of secondary education, after his family had been moved on to Penrith.

Secondary Education at Goulburn

In 1906 Rev. Charles Jones again received 'marching orders' in the Lord's service from the Methodist Conference, but this time the peripatetic family did not have so far to move. Between 1906 and 1909 young Frank Jones worked at his secondary school studies at the established inland town of Goulburn, almost directly across the rugged Australian alpine chain from Kiama. A convenient main road linking the coastal route with the interior passed from Cooma through Queanbeyan and Bungendore to Goulburn. Goulburn had been a flourishing settlement in convict days, and was long a supply centre for pastoralists of the inland plains country as well as those of the chilly high country to the south-east, known as the Monaro. The climate of Goulburn was a cross between that of Wagga Wagga and Orange, exhibiting the searing dry and dusty heat of an inland summer, but also prone to frosty nights and freezing winter winds from the snow-capped mountains situated not far to its east and south. Frank Hackett-Jones many years later reminisced that the boys of Goulburn experienced fewer sexual fantasies in that land of cool winds, than had their equivalents in Kiama's more luxuriant coastal climate. Perhaps that explains something of the long-term frightening effects of the hell-fire preaching of the minister of Jamberoo on impressionable growing boys.

Rev. Charles Jones was back on familiar ground. The old goldmining centre of Adelong in the nearby high country, and the plains village of Crookwell to the north-west (in each of which he had once served his church dutifully) were within Goulburn's mercantile sphere of interest. Wagga Wagga and Deniliquin, which also held so many important memories for him, were again within reach. Goulburn might lack the rich arable soil of Orange or Kiama, but it was the centre for a widely spread and significant pastoral and agricultural area. It was also an important railway junction linking what we know as the Canberra district or The Australian Capital Territory, via a railway that connected the high Monaro to the main Sydney to Melbourne line. Goulburn had long been an important highway town for traffic travelling between Sydney and the fertile river lands of the Riverina, or even on to Melbourne and the once-famed Victorian goldfield towns. The town of Goulburn had developed greatly since its convict days, and well before the end of the 19th century it boasted impressive Anglican and Roman Catholic stone cathedrals. Apparently, the town also boasted more than one Methodist church, Rev. Charles Jones being minister to Goulburn's flourishing Goldsmith Street congregation.

Between 1906 and 1909 young Frank Jones passed through his main period of adolescence (thirteen to sixteen years) at Goulburn's State secondary school, then popularly but unofficially known as a 'High School'. The two highest classes were dubbed High School, but were in fact training classes for entry to the State's educational service. Senior students were called 'probationary students', and they received books and a small second-year money allowance from the State. Ideas of a scholarship to the prestigious Sydney Boys' High School were abandoned, as young Frank appeared to flourish in his rural High School setting. Already, Frank was being guided towards a teaching career, although he had no personal leanings in that direction. In 1908 he duly became a 'probationary student', and received a sound general education in the traditional humanities subjects with the addition of a little basic science and carpentry. Frank Jones was dux of Goulburn High School in 1908, and this fanned his latent academic ambitions. At that stage he bought himself a Greek grammar for private study, and in later years confessed to having had an exaggerated idea of his own student abilities. Already, he was dreaming of going on to Sydney University and becoming a professor of something or other interesting.[4]

In that era, universities were still very much places reserved for the rich and privileged classes of society, but by following the path of teacher training it was possible to obtain university qualifications without paying those university fees that were beyond the pocket of a Methodist minister. The rural peer group at Goulburn's State secondary school exhibited no great ambitions, nor visions of a glorious personal future. The high-fliers were happy to take teacher or bank clerk appointments, such employment appearing to offer physical ease and security to boys whose family finances were usually tied to the vagaries of droughts and summer bushfires, and to the ever-doubtful value of next season's crop or wool clip.

The Rev. Charles Jones, always conscious of the devil and his wiles with a weak humanity, was opposed to bank employment because it required that a man might not marry until he received a salary of £200 a year, which in practice meant middle age. Apart from the temptations of such enforced celibacy, there were the ever-present lures of the enticing contents of a well-endowed bank till, encouraging lowly-paid employees 'to dip their fingers in'. Rev. Charles Jones never underestimated these temptations of the devil. He had probably known them too well. At one stage young Frank considered the Indian Civil Service as a possible future career, little dreaming that 'accident' would later lead him to almost a lifetime of toil in the less exotic New South Wales Public Service.

The father spoke little when not in the pulpit, but took his son with him on occasional shooting expeditions into the surrounding countryside. Rev. Charles Jones usually used a Winchester .22 rifle, presumably on rabbits, while young Frank was occasionally privileged to use the more cumbersome and noisy double-barrelled shot gun for closer-range targets. Frank enjoyed football and cricket with friends in a paddock adjacent to the parsonage, and could also retreat to the impressive two-storey brick stables for practice at woodwork. Although a Methodist minister was not a wealthy man, in a country town like Goulburn he was a man of considerable social standing, and his accommodation and transport facilities were such as many townspeople might envy. The horses used by John Wesley on his grinding missionary tours around England had never grown fat on the job, nor did those of Wesley's Antipodean successors travelling in pursuit of lost souls.

'Lost souls' often dropped in at the parsonage around sunset, which was the time of day when travelling swagmen were thinking of a warm and dry camp for the night. If they did not arrive too early, they would not have much daylight to sweat at the woodheap in return for the meagre ration of bread tea and sugar customarily dispensed according to bush tradition. The residences of clergymen were always considered a soft touch by such old hands of the roads, and those large two-storeyed stable buildings doubtless provided comfortable quarters for the night. Equally comfortable in the mind of young Frank Jones were the quiet and musty reading rooms of the local Mechanic's Institute Library, where he eagerly perused a range of general reading matter. These country libraries were usually organised by a little core of local professional men, and they contributed much to the education of many serious-minded young country boys of that generation. This solid reading would be a preparation for studies at Sydney Boys' High School, at the Sydney Teachers' College, and at Sydney University.[5]

CHAPTER 3

UNIVERSITY AND PUBLIC SERVICE: 1909 TO 1916

Early in 1909 Rev. Charles Jones was informed that his next Methodist charge was to be at Penrith, well to the west of Sydney and not far from the famed Blue Mountains, but sufficiently close (by rail) to New South Wales' major institutions of higher learning that his son Frank would be able to take advantage of them. From April 1909 Frank, nearing the end of his 16th year, began to learn something of life in the city after years of relatively isolated rural existence.

Even today, the broader environs of Penrith include wide open spaces. Early last century those environs were definitely rural. One of the best-known autobiographical works produced in Australia in recent decades is that entitled *Caddie: a Sydney Barmaid*. Caddie also spent her earliest years at Penrith near the beginning of this century, and she described it as 'a small town about thirty miles west of Sydney, which sprawled untidily almost at the foot of the Blue Mountains'. Furthermore, 'it was a dreary place, scorching heat in the summer and bitter cold in the winter'. It is most likely that Caddie had 'gone bush' with her family, before young Frank Jones arrived on the Penrith scene. Even had the girl still been there, it is unlikely that her paths would have crossed those of Frank Jones living quietly at the Methodist parsonage, and intent on academic conquests in the city

Allan Hackett Jones at Penrith Parsonage, 1909

of Sydney. Initially, Frank continued his earlier Probationary Student Teacher studies at Sydney Boys' High School.[1]

During those years between 1909 and 1912, when the young Frank Jones was pursuing his higher educational aims in Sydney, much was changing in the New South Wales educational system. The State secondary education system was undergoing a process of transition, and significant changes were also occurring in Sydney's teacher-training facilities. In the year 1910 there were five State High Schools for the whole of New South Wales: Sydney Boys' High, Sydney Girls' High, Maitland Boys High, Maitland Girls High, and Newcastle High School. These had a total enrolment of 1,168 students, and an average daily attendance of only 826 students. From early in 1911 the senior sections of Fort Street School were also formed into High Schools, to be known as Fort Street Boy's High School, and Fort Street Girls' High School.[2]

At the beginning of this century Sydney Boys' High School occupied the only building in New South Wales that had been specifically designed for use as a high school, although it was situated in a noisy industrial area not likely to provide ideal study conditions. Solidly built from stone and brick, the school had seven classrooms. It did not possess any laboratories, nor a library, or even a proper assembly room. Science students were expected to undertake any laboratory experiments at the adjacent Sydney Technical College. One of Sydney High's prominent teachers early this century, the Scot C. R. Smith, has been described as teaching Latin, Greek, French and German:

> moving quietly among groups of boys, some of them studying Greek, others German, and each divided into small groups according to the grade they had reached.

The teaching and learning process thus described was taking place in a room that was also used as the school's assembly hall. The school day at Sydney Boys' High School consisted of five teaching periods, each lesson being of one hour's duration.[3]

Major changes in the State's High School system occurred a little too late for Frank Jones and his parents to take advantage of them. From the beginning of 1911 the State High School course changed from a three-year to a four-year schedule, the Leaving Certificate being the final goal of this educational programme. More importantly from the perspective of a Methodist parsonage, fees were abolished. In 1910, of the total £11,530 that High School education cost the State of New South Wales, £3,598 had come from students' fees. A little later again, in 1912, New South Wales' Labor Premier William Holman established a school bursary system intended to provide the opportunity for any child in the State's secondary education system, 'regardless of sex or sect', to qualify for free tuition at Sydney University. It is possible that such provisions, had they come a little earlier, might have dissuaded young Frank Jones from becoming 'bonded' to the Department of Public Instruction in order to obtain a free university education. The long-term consequence of that 'teaching bond' was to be a working life largely spent in the New South Wales Public Service.[4]

Frank's sojourn in the Probationary Student Teachers' class at Sydney Boys' High School was very brief. He enjoyed the fast train ride between Penrith and Sydney, returning home after 5 o'clock each evening. Despite physical disabilities involving his feet and his eyesight, he made the most of the school's sporting life. Frank played Rugby Union football with Sydney High School's Second Team, which he much later described as the weakest team in the Great

Public Schools Competition. Penrith's parsonage possessed the luxury of a tennis court, and young Frank was sufficiently enthusiastic about tennis to walk six miles to Mt Druitt for a game.

The Reluctant Teacher

In the second term of 1909 Frank Jones passed the examinations required for entry to Sydney Teachers' Training College, and by third term he was attending Penrith Public School for teaching practice sessions. He was conscious of being a solitary, studious soul, and did not find it easy to make new friends. Among Frank's closest friends at that time were members of the Hall family who lived at Emu Plains, some of whom attended Sydney Boys' High School.

Mr Hall was a one-time Methodist minister who had made the mistake of being 'converted' to Henry George's Single Tax Land Tax theory. It is not difficult to understand why a struggling Methodist minister might be attracted by a theory that advocated breaking up large landholdings for distribution among the people. Given the make-up of rural or semi-rural congregations, neither is it difficult to understand how he came to lose his congregation and be left high and dry by the Church. Without the assistance of Henry George's system, Mr Hall had solved his problem of enforced retirement by growing strawberries. Frank enjoyed Christmas vacations with the Hall boys, sometimes at a cave camp on the banks of the fast-flowing Nepean River. Among the sons of Mr Hall was one boy, also named Frank, who would later become a professor in the United States.

The young Frank Jones was attracted to more than one of these families of equally devout parentage to his own, with children of unusual intellectual or artistic abilities. The Muscio family possessed a vineyard near St Mary's, not far from Penrith. Among the sons was one Bernard, who then taught philosophy from his base at St Andrew's College in the University of Sydney. His sister Dorothy promised to be a musical prodigy, but her Swiss puritan father refused to let her take the risk of being depraved by overexposure to music. Another son, Theo, was Frank's age, but he had settled for the safer context of an orchardist's life.[5]

During the year 1910 Frank Jones was introduced to life at Sydney Teachers' College. A new era had begun at the College in 1907 when Alexander Mackie was appointed its Principal. With the support of his board Mackie had his college established in the university grounds, the aim being to staff the State's secondary schools with university graduates. Prior to 1911, students came there to be taught primary school teaching only. Although the best of the Teachers' College students were sent to the University of Sydney, no special training was then provided for teaching in secondary schools. Principal Mackie, who also occupied the office of Professor of Education at Sydney University, received the princely salary of £800 per annum for his services. His assistant, the College's Vice-Principal Dr P.R. Cole, earned £450 per year. There were twenty other lecturers and assistants, each earning somewhere between £120 and £350 a year. Frank Jones was impressed by other skills of his Principal and Vice-Principal, not directly related to their teaching profession. Himself a somewhat shy lad where ladies were concerned, he noted that two female student teachers of his era at the College would later become wives to the Principal and Vice-Principal.[6]

Frank's introduction to life at Sydney Teachers' College was not designed to appeal to a studious recluse. Along with other 'freshers' he underwent college initiation by having his head shoved under a tap of free-flowing cold water. It was then that Rev. Charles Jones signed a substantial money bond that committed young Frank to teach for at least three years on completion of his studies. There were four groups of trainee teachers in Frank's year, each consisting of thirty-five persons, with slightly more male students than female students. In breadth of coverage, the curriculum was extensive. Each group took one language subject, one science, one history, one theory of education subject, and Frank's group chose to study Latin and Chemistry. Pupils studied English, Geography Mathematics, Hygiene and Singing, in order to teach others across the whole (non-technical) State educational curriculum. There were also teaching-practice sessions at various Sydney schools: doubtless not easy for a shy and retiring boy, who had spent much of his life hitherto in rural parsonages.

At this time, the young Frank Jones lived at a Lewisham Boarding House that was run by family friends from his days at Orange, the Wallis family. Long accustomed to being top of the class in small schools and dux of his country schools at both primary and secondary levels, the academically ambitious boy received a blow to his pride when he passed his annual Teachers' College examination, but at number eight position on the graded list. Nevertheless, he had qualified to matriculate at the University of Sydney, and that had been his main ambition for years. Other aspects of life in 'the big city' also amazed him, including the sight of grown men students dancing together in the College Common Room at lunchtimes, to the varied strains of waltzes, polkas and mazurkas.

In his second year at Sydney Teachers' College, Frank's course broadened out from the basic lectures in education at the College and teaching-practice sessions in schools, to include first-year studies directed towards the Bachelor of Arts Degree at Sydney University. Frank's academic self-confidence, nurtured through years of being a big fish in a small rural educational pool, had not yet taken a real beating. He set out to pursue a university course that included honours studies in Philosophy, English, and Latin, as well as private studies (at a pass level) in Greek.

Those Greek studies were of special significance to the young university freshman. Frank was then driven by what he later described as 'a romantic notion' of becoming an archaeologist. Almost certainly, that interest related to the archaeological enthusiasms of his favourite uncle, James Thompson Hackett, the only surviving full-brother to his beloved mother. J.T. Hackett was almost a father to Frank, and took a deep interest in the digs being conducted by prominent British academics in

Lizzie Jane Hackett with her brother James

James Thompson Hackett

Egypt. He eventually died at Luxor while accompanying one such archaeological expedition led by Professor Sayce.

Although Frank Hackett-Jones later described his own early archaeological ambitions as unrealistic, it is not surprising that a son of the parsonage in that era should have such interests. Many of the diggings were in ancient lands closely allied to the worlds of those Jewish and Christian Scriptures that had been a part of his home life and mental furnishings since infancy. Many clerical families considered studies in Greek language (whether of the Classical or New Testament eras) fundamental to a proper education. Young Frank, the shy but aspiring 'boy from the bush', was cruelly unlucky to be exposed to the student competition of one who must rate among Australia's intellectual giants, of truly international stature.[7]

For an ordinary student of above-average ability, aspiring to competence in languages and archaeological studies, the competition provided by one Vere Gordon Childe at Sydney University was more than daunting. As the aged Frank Hackett-Jones ruefully remembered, in his first year at Sydney University Childe lectured the Classical Association on the subject of ancient Sanskrit. Young Frank Jones felt cut down to size, and promptly abandoned both his Greek studies and his archaeological ambitions.

He need not have felt so mortified. V.G. Childe, who was also the son of a Sydney clergyman, was a prodigy of unusual proportions. He was not the only student of unusual genius then attending the University of Sydney. Many years later, the matured Frank Jones would return to the University of Sydney to be educated for the role of a barrister and solicitor, and among his revered teachers would be Sir John Peden, Professor of Law. At about that time one Herbert Vere Evatt would make headlines by becoming Australia's youngest-ever High Court Judge, despite the handicap of a suspect left wing political background.

While Frank Jones and Gordon Childe first attended Sydney University, prior to World War I, Professor John Peden was revelling in the extraordinary academic potential of the young Herbert Vere Evatt. Evatt had passed out of Fort Street School at the end of 1911, having been its Captain and Senior Prefect. Up at the University of Sydney Evatt took any prizes that were offering. It mattered little whether the field was mathematics, English, philosophy, or law. One of the few who could compete academically with Evatt was V.G. Childe, who remained a lifelong friend of 'the Doc'.[8]

Although Frank Jones and Gordon Childe were each the sons of Protestant clergymen, initially with a common interest in ancient languages and archaeology, their personalities were poles apart and they could never have achieved real communication. Childe was an intellectual rebel, self-confident in his mental powers and well-known around the university where he might often be found in loud debate with Bert Evatt. Frank Jones, on the other hand, remained true to his Methodist parsonage conditioning: socially and politically unquestioning and conservative, with no impulse to query the middle-class values of the staid world in which he grew up. Nevertheless, as he later confessed, he had a furtive admiration for outspoken young intellectual rebels who dared damnation in the pursuit of knowledge and wisdom.

All his long life, Frank Jones would struggle with (or against) the mental and spiritual domination of his earliest Methodist upbringing, whereas Gordon Childe put his respectable religious background right behind him from student days, and became one of the 20th century's most innovative scholars; one whose thinking unashamedly acknowledged a considerable input from the thought of Karl Marx.

Despite losing his place as Vice-Principal of St Andrew's College (with assured academic standing within the University of Sydney) for freely expounding doctrines of philosophical and political heresy, Childe would battle on to the top of the international academic tree. His early contacts in the New South Wales Labor movement were sometimes invaluable. It was the influence of the young William McKell, another Sydney contemporary who was assisted in his (non-university) struggle to gain legal qualifications by Childe, that would get Childe back to a minor government job in London. Childe had been desperate for any opportunity to pursue his intellectual ambitions in Europe, after being rejected in his home city. Although that posting was spitefully taken away from him by the incoming Nationalist Government in New South Wales, Childe would overcome all the obstacles put in his path to spend thirty-six years abroad in respected academic positions.

William McKell, the novice working class would-be lawyer whom Childe had helped to obtain basic educational qualifications, would become Premier of New South Wales, and ultimately Governor General of Australia. A much older Frank Jones (by then Frank Hackett-Jones) would complete his career in the New South Wales Public Service as the legal officer to McKell's favourite political hobby horse: the New South Wales Housing Commission.

V.G. Childe would be invited to become foundation Professor of Archaeology at Edinburgh University, and would be awarded degrees for his research in archaeology, anthropology and the social sciences, by a wide range of revered institutions including Harvard, Oslo, Oxford, and London Universities. In 1957, brought back to Australia as a guest of the Commonwealth Government, Childe was awarded the degree of Doctor of Letters by the University of Sydney, largely at the instigation of his lifelong friend Dr H.V. Evatt. Later that year Childe died tragically as a result of a cliff-top fall in those beloved Blue Mountains that he (and Frank Jones too) had so often tramped. Had the young Frank Jones realised the stature of the man against whom he measured himself academically prior to World War I, he might not so readily have abandoned his driving linguistic and archaeological ambitions. Childe would be widely recognised as the most significant archaeologist of the 20th century.[9]

Feeling demoralised, and overpowered by the heavy academic programme that he had set himself on top of his considerable teacher-training obligations, the youthful Frank Jones changed direction towards being a drop-out of Sydney University during 1911. He gave up his honours ambitions, dodged his second Greek examination, and spent many happy hours on the tennis courts. Despite the blow to his initial life's plan, Frank retained many happy memories of that year at the University of Sydney. In particular, he long retained respectful memories of his teachers there. By 1912 his university studies had been cut down to size to match his deflated ego: part-time evening classes in English and Geology only.

The University of Sydney at that time was not such a large institution as the one we know today. In 1911, 1,387 students attended some lectures there, and these included 194 intrepid females who 'dared to know'. There were almost as many academic staff as there were ladies. The eighteen professors listed as present in 1912 included one Colonel H. J. Foster, R.E., 'Director of Military Science'.[10] He is not so well remembered as men like McCallum, or Peden, who helped shape generations of young minds at Sydney University, including that of Frank Jones. The logical rigour of a Peden did not fit easily with the unquestioning piety of Frank's youth, and for much of his adult life he remained torn between those two 'spiritual homes': the Methodist Church and the University of Sydney.

Although Frank's university ambitions were fast dwindling during 1911, that 'teaching bond' which his father had signed as an entry ticket to the university's higher academic studies was still very much a reality. He had never been driven by any serious desire to teach in schools, but at the age of twenty years Frank had to face up to the realities of life as a school teacher. His first teaching job was at Enmore Primary School, where he had a class of approximately fifty boys of about ten years of age. His teaching subjects were varied, and included French, chemistry and even singing. That broad Sydney Teachers' College vocational training was proving its worth. Frank Jones never regarded singing as his personal strongpoint, but he had a singing class of 150 assorted voices to control. He sidestepped the normal disciplinary problems of such a situation by allowing them to sing pop songs of that era. The children intoned lustily, the time passed safely, and nobody was sufficiently aware or interested to interfere with Frank's 'singing lessons'.

The children whom Frank taught at Enmore Primary School were not highly motivated towards books and learning, as he had always been. Few of their homes would have contained the well-stocked English classical library of Frank's early parsonage settings. Most of the Enmore students made no secret of the fact that they were merely filling in time until they reached the legal school-leaving age of fourteen years. Depressed by this lack of interest in learning, Frank quickly came to the conclusion that the life of a schoolteacher was no more his vocation than was that of an archaeologist. In order to avoid payment of that 'bond' held by the State's education authorities, Frank decided to enter for the New South Wales Public Service Examinations. However, Enmore students indirectly foiled this initial escape move too – they infected Frank with a severe attack of measles. Upon recovery, he was afflicted with chronic catarrh, and was unable to sit the examination.[11]

At that time the parental home moved again, but not so very far. In 1913 Rev. Charles Jones was not being called to yet another triennial parish task by the Methodist Conference. He had reached retirement age, and had decided to return to the district setting into which he had been born in 1844. The Jones retirement retreat was a farmlet of four acres at North Parramatta. Even in retirement, the energetic old minister of God remained active in his Church's affairs, and he prepared a regular Sunday sermon on the night before his death.[12]

Although Parramatta had changed greatly from its situation in 1844 when New South Wales' convict-assignment system had only very recently been abolished, the wider Parramatta district had not yet been swallowed up by an expanding metropolis and in 1913 was still largely rural.

In the Korean War era, Frank Hackett-Jones would emulate his father by himself choosing a retirement setting on a small (although considerably larger) New South Wales farm. Even when entering his tenth decade of life, in distant Adelaide, he would still dearly love to till the soil of his extensive orchard garden. He was to spend most of his life working in cities, but Frank Jones' abiding interests were shaped by an early rural or semi-rural upbringing.

The young Frank Jones moved residence with his parents not long before his twenty-first birthday, and accordingly briefly applied his teaching skills at Auburn's State primary school. From that earlier North Parramatta farmlet home, young Frank made a second attempt at sitting the New South Wales Public Service Examinations, and on this occasion the fates were kinder to him. An escape route from the State's education service was opened, without the financial penalties that would have ensued for his retired father had Frank left the State's service altogether.

Salvation in the Public Service

Although Frank Jones was not long employed at Auburn's school, some of his later public service work would be carried out under the indirect control of a more widely known Auburn identity. One Jack Lang was in 1913 making his way in the world as a shrewd-headed Auburn Real Estate Agent. Well prior to World War I, Lang was already a successful businessman and active leader in the local Starr-Bowkett Co-operative Building Society. Much of Frank Jones' first phase of public service work would be in those sections of the New South Wales Bureau of Statistics that supervised the activities of friendly societies and co-operative societies. In the later 1920s, when Jack Lang ('the Big Fella') was well on his way to achieving notoriety as Premier of New South Wales, Frank Jones would have risen slowly through the ranks to the position of Inspector of Co-operative Societies in a Bureau of Statistics that was at times under Lang's direct ministerial control.

Although by instinct socially and politically conservative, for much of his (interrupted) working life in the New South Wales Public Service, Frank Jones would operate in spheres that were dear to the hearts of political ministerial guides belonging to the Labor Party. During the 1930s, when conservative politicians did rule the State Parliamentary roost of New South Wales for almost a decade, Frank would be involved in legal studies and the life of a small-time Sydney barrister operating outside the Public Service.

CHAPTER 4

FRANK JONES GOES TO WAR:
1916 TO 1919

For decades, the official New South Wales Public Service Lists would indicate that Frank Harold Jones had first entered the service on 22 January 1912. That entrance date apparently referred to his first official recognition as an employee of the Department of Public Instruction, while a teacher at Enmore. Frank himself always considered that his real entry to the State Public Service occurred on 1 September 1913, when he became a junior clerk in the New South Wales Bureau of Statistics.[1] Even an appointment to such a junior position in the State Public Service was an event worthy of notice in the *New South Wales Government Gazette* of that era:

> Special Gazette under the Public Service Act, 1902. His Excellency the Governor, with the advice of the Executive Council, and upon the recommendation of the Public Service Board, has approved, in pursuance of the provisions of the Public Service Act, 1902, of the appointment of Mr Frank Harold Jones, ex-student, Public School, Auburn, as Junior Clerk, Bureau of Statistics and Registry of Friendly Societies and Trade Unions, on probation (vice J.A. Byrne, transferred), to take effect from the date of commencing duty.[2]

That official fanfare appears rather excessive in the light of the modest realities to which it related. However, it cannot be doubted that Frank Harold Jones had properly arrived in the New South Wales Public Service by September 1913. As a junior school teacher, although apparently recognised as belonging to the Public Service for the purposes of his service record, Frank had not yet undertaken the Public Service Examinations, and appears to have received no recognition whatsoever in the *Government Gazette*.

During these first three decades of the 20th century, when the young Frank Jones was finding his feet in the educational and public-service institutions of New South Wales' coastal metropolis, the Labor Party began to attract attention both at State and Federal political levels. Between October 1910 and June 1913, J.S.T. McGowan's Labor Government ruled New South Wales. The Ministers of Public Instruction in that Labor Government during Frank's brief teaching phase were G.S. Beeby and Fred Flowers. The Premier, McGowan, died at about the time that Frank Jones was transferring from his post as teacher under the Department of Public Instruction, to his new role as Bureau of Statistics clerk under the oversight of the Chief Secretary's Department.

Thus it was that when Frank Jones made his entry to the Public Service proper, later in 1913, the Labor Premier of New South Wales was the eminent and controversial W.A. Holman. By late 1916, when Holman fell foul of the Labor Party and (like his colleague W.M. Hughes at the Federal Labor level) departed from his Party over the issue of conscription for overseas war service, Frank Jones had succeeded in his struggle to join the First Australian Imperial Force. Only very briefly, upon his return from war service in 1919, would Frank Jones work in a political environment shaped by W. A. Holman's hybrid government of ex-Labor men and Nationalists that governed New South Wales from November 1916 to April 1920. In that administration the Nationalist Party leader, G.W. Fuller, ran the Colonial Secretary's Department under whose umbrella Frank worked.[3]

Although entry to the Public Service proper had solved the Jones family problem of how to avoid payment of Frank's 'teaching bond', it had not really solved the more serious long-term problem of what Frank wanted to do with his life. With his appointment to the Registry of Friendly Societies in New South Wales' Bureau of Statistics in September 1913 went a temporary abandonment of those earlier much-cherished university study ambitions. From teaching listless working class children, Frank found himself involved in the tedium of examining annual friendly-society returns to government, actuarial valuation work, and the manipulation of primitive manual calculating machines. All this stimulating activity took place in an old three-storey terrace block in Young Street, Sydney. At that time Thomas Waites was Chief Clerk, and Frank found him a congenial boss. Waites was a fine athlete, and encouraged his sports-loving junior clerk to undertake physical culture lessons from Georges Dupain.

The Government Statistician, Registrar and Actuary of Friendly Societies in charge of the Bureau of Statistics at that time was John B. Trivett, F.R.A.S., F.S.S. Prior to an Act of the New South Wales Parliament of 1899, the State's friendly societies had operated under the terms of an Act of 1873, and under the provisions of that earlier Act it had proved impossible to obtain adequate accurate details about friendly society memberships to formulate actuarial tables specifically related to New South Wales conditions. Prior to 1910, New South Wales friendly societies had to calculate their risks of life and sickness payouts, and related membership fees, on the information in actuarial tables based upon the experience of England's Manchester Unity organisation. At the time when Frank Jones first entered the Bureau of Statistics, that situation was changing. The passage of the 1899 Act ensured:

> ample powers of compulsion to ensure prompt and accurate returns relating to all the operations of the Societies; so that the means became available whereby in the course of time it would be feasible to collect the data upon which to establish tables representative of a purely local experience, and to derive the requisite Mortality and Sickness Tables for the use of the actuary in the valuations of the risks contracted by the Friendly Societies of New South Wales.[4]

When one contemplates the tedium involved (for a pre-computer generation) in the manipulation of data for the formulation of actuarial tables, then it is not hard to see why a young man like Frank Jones would fail to be attracted to the actuary's lifestyle. As a junior clerk, he would have been involved in many hours of monotonous data processing of friendly societies' statistics. The New South Wales Bureau of Statistics possessed cards relating to every member of the numerous friendly-society branches scattered across town and country:

The details given in the annual returns furnished by the various societies, and relating to each individual, are recorded on cards, which thus furnish a complete history of each Society as to its attendant risks. On these cards are stated the year of birth and of entry ... the mode of exit and year of exit ... through death, clearance, secession ...

Mining communities of New South Wales were treated under a separate category, their risks of illness and death being significantly higher than those for 'ordinary' citizens.[5]

The New South Wales Public Service had earlier undergone some reform, in the interests of greater efficiency, but the young junior clerk was not highly impressed by the efficiency of the organisation of which he was now part. In his old age Frank Hackett-Jones remembered an 'easygoing office' with 'a Dickensian staff'. He reminisced that it was a working environment in which it was easy to get a reputation for energy and initiative, but because promotion was by order of seniority, it was much harder to obtain a salary appropriate to one's input of energy and initiative: 'for years I was too young'.

Viewing F.H. Jones' advancing financial situation through the medium of the Public Service Lists, it is not apparent that he was so hardly done by. Salaries are always relative, but a junior clerk in the public service (especially in a department that did not press him too hard) enjoyed a job security and ever-rising assured salary that would have been the envy of many fellow New South Welshmen, in city or country. Those earliest years prior to his departure with the AIF in 1916 were doubtless lowly paid. Initially, on his return to work in 1919, his salary was only £195 per year, but for a young and single man that sum was not too depressing. Average male earnings in Sydney in 1919 were in the vicinity of £200 per year. By 1928, when average male earnings were around the £267 mark, according to the Public Service Lists F.H. Jones was earning £550, and still single.[6]

In 1914, with World War about to disrupt his secure office environment, the young and aspiring public servant was not finding life too uncomfortable. He still travelled into the city each day from his parents' Parramatta retirement address, and he enjoyed lunches at the Domain Baths, along with a swim. In spare hours at North Parramatta he built an ant-bed tennis court, collecting conveniently adjacent ant-bed material in his father's wheelbarrow. In

Seymour, Pennant Hills Road, Parramatta – Frank Jones' parents' home during his twenties

August 1914 the first rumblings of what would degenerate into the Great War were heard. At first it caused little excitement in the family home. It was regarded as a storm in a teacup that would soon be over, and there was no need to think about personal involvement.

Even after the bloody assault on Gallipoli's uninviting beachhead in April 1915, it took time for the message to sink in at Sydney. In May 1915, Sydney's *Bulletin* could still reproach Australians for their cheerful unconcern in the face of what was obviously a much more death-dealing conflict than people had realised. That situation changed as the serious message of the Gallipoli casualty lists sank in. In July 1915, 75,000 Australian troops had departed abroad, and 17,000 more were in training to go. By October 1915 there were 74,000 men being trained for war. Frank Jones was wrenched from the security and ease of the Bureau of Statistics by news of the deaths of some of his own acquaintance. Given his solid Protestant family background and the war propaganda then emanating from such sources, it is not surprising that he should feel the urge to participate in this great act of sacrifice for the Empire.[7]

Despite his love of sport, Frank had long suffered the disadvantages of acute short-sightedness, and this defect initially foiled his strong desire to fight abroad with the AIF. Apart from his later legal interests, Frank Jones had little in common with his Sydney contemporary, H.V. Evatt. However, they would both be barred from the AIF in 1915 because of defective vision, which was in each case probably aggravated by long hours of study in poorly-lit conditions. Whereas Evatt wore a 'rejection button' on his lapel (to his mother's disgust) there is no record that Frank Jones was so ostentatiously disappointed. Evatt's later great rival from Victoria, R.G. Menzies, was at that time defending the ranks of those who, like him, 'stayed at home' in a period of patriotic frenzy. In such a situation it took considerable moral courage for a Protestant to take that position; although Menzies would still be affected by the resultant guilt near the end of his political career, when he introduced national conscription for service in Vietnam. Frank Jones, like Bert Evatt, was very frustrated in his driving desire for personal sacrifice.

Rejection at the Army recruiting centre meant that it was to be business as usual at the Registry of Friendly Societies office. The Government Statistician was at that time indicating displeasure with the performance of his official actuary, and Frank as junior clerk was asked to study towards an actuarial degree. This had usually meant study in Britain, and there was only a correspondence course available to Sydney residents. The junior clerk found this a poor alternative to opportunities for self-sacrifice on the imperial altar, and soon found actuarial studies were too tedious and boring for his liking. Anyway, he had no desire to spend his life bent over a manual calculator, like the much-abused official actuary. However, if he was to rise through the ranks of clerks to higher things, he obviously did need specialised qualifications of some sort.

At that point a friend persuaded him to try accountancy, which would prove to be much more to Frank's liking. However, just as his accountancy coach (R.D. Bogan) found him an appropriate accountancy position, the eyesight test was lowered for men desiring to join the Australian Medical Corps or the Australian Service Corps. The surging demand for cannon fodder for Europe was breaking down the original highly demanding physical fitness requirements of the Australian Military Forces. Frank Jones again saw his opportunity for glorious sacrifice, and, having been once deprived, he clutched at it.

Frank Jones showed more initiative than his more academically talented contemporary, Bert Evatt. By 1916 recruits for specific army jobs were required only to read the top three lines of each eye-test chart, but they were not allowed to wear glasses. At the recruiting depot attended by Frank Jones, recruits were expected to read the top three lines of three different charts. Although Frank's short-sightedness was so acute as to have made this an impossible task, his memory was sufficiently good for him to memorise the charts through a convenient window while still in possession of his thick-lens glasses. Perhaps the AIF thought that anybody with a memory like that should be capable of some service to the military machine. More likely, by 1916 the demand for reinforcements was so strong that the authorities were not too serious about finding reasons to reject volunteers. Anyway, that reluctant public servant, F.H. Jones, had finally found a vocation more suited to the romantic aspirations of young manhood. Nothing, except the army bureaucracy, now stood between Frank and his instincts for self-immolation on the imperial altar.[8]

Even when entering his nineties, Frank Hackett-Jones still felt the passion of what it had meant to risk the ultimate personal sacrifice in 1916. He remained impatient of those who wrote of the 'uselessness' and 'waste' of the attack on Gallipoli. The author on one occasion put it to him that near the end of the 20th century (given the horrendous nature of modern martial technology) a major war could have no winners, and had therefore lost any point it might once have had. The old soldier replied that 'war always had been mad'. However, that urge to self-sacrifice in a national and imperial cause that had driven him in 1916 remained a symptom of virtuous 'idealism': a quality that Frank believed to be sadly lacking in the Australian community of his latter years. To abandon comfort and sanitation, and to let one's body become a prey to fleas and lice, was still considered a splendid thing.

Frank always remained convinced that any self-respecting person would have done what he did, despite his chronic short-sightedness and feet problems that made route-marching torture for him. In order to understand that conviction, we need to realise that the Australian Protestant society in which Frank Jones had been reared understood the military cause in 1916-17 as a holy war against the forces of evil, personified by Kaiser Wilhelm of Germany and his steel-helmeted hordes of 'Huns'. Not all of those who volunteered, especially in the mindlessly romantic mood of 1914, were driven by such ideals of self-sacrifice. Many were country boys who recognised a rare opportunity to see exotic far-away places at government expense.

Before too many months had passed, Frank Jones would see plenty of sacrifice all around him, as whole companies of Australian and New Zealand soldiers were decimated by malaria in the Middle East. However, on passing that all-important medical examination for entry to the AIF, Frank Jones did not yet understand how much more struggle there would be before he realised his ambition of getting close enough to the enemy to make self-sacrifice a real probability. Much of the story of Trooper F.H. Jones' participation in 'the war to end all wars' is the record of a conscientious private soldier's struggle to put himself in the place of sacrifice, in the face of a military organisation that appears to have considered this urgent ambition a thing to be thwarted at all costs.

F.H. Jones ceased to be a public servant and became a private soldier when he entered Liverpool Army Camp in March 1916. To mark this important change in lifestyle, the new recruit was issued with his regulation dungarees. The novice soldier's first experience has been shared by many military recruits before and since. He was supplied with a jacket size 3, and trousers size 7, whereas his body shape required both jacket and trousers to be size 5. There was the symbolic slouch hat of the digger, together with solid-hide military boots and heavy socks, and an issue of flannel shirts and underwear. The new recruit was also supplied with one rubber ground sheet, a mattress cover, and a modest quantity of straw to convert the latter item into a functional army mattress. Recruits soon came to appreciate that straw packing, as they slept on ground sheets stretched over bare ground (hollowed out to the shape of a hip) in their six-man Bell tents.

Service on the Home Front

The opportunity for self-sacrifice of an unexpected kind presented itself much more rapidly than the young recruit had

Frank Hackett-Jones and his mother, prior to enlistment, about 1916

imagined possible. He was transferred to Milson Island Venereal Diseases Hospital on the Hawkesbury River, after only four days at Liverpool Camp. There the innocent son of a Methodist parsonage was confronted by 600 patients who were undergoing treatment for the ravages of gonorrhoea and syphilis, presumably largely as a result of the delights of the flesh lavished upon fee-paying Anzacs in the backstreet brothels of Cairo. Apart from the unattractiveness of the medical challenge presented by the damaged bodies of those inhabitants of Milson Island's Venereal Diseases Hospital, the attendants' camp was situated close to a piggery, and there were fleas galore.

Fortunately, one weekend a fortnight was allowed for leave from the monotony of gonorrhoea, syphilis, and fleas. It took approximately six weeks for Frank's full military uniform to arrive, and by that time he could feel a real Anzac, however unexpected his particular form of contribution to the imperial war effort. The young soldier was not dismayed when, after ten weeks of loyal service to the Australian army's most immediate medical needs, a call came for soldiers of the king prepared to volunteer for return to Liverpool Camp. Here was a test of the desire of young Australian manhood to serve the nation at the front. Frank Jones' choice was crystal clear: 'I joined in the rush'. Presumably, another batch of fresh recruits were due to get their warning about the fleshpots of Egypt and Sydney.

Domestic duties at Liverpool Camp also offered opportunities for sacrifices of a sort that had not previously filled the imagination of the eager young volunteer. As the son of a god-fearing parsonage, Frank Jones was accustomed to a domestic situation where the chores of housekeeping were carried out without any need for the males of the household to notice. Private Jones realised that he was not cut out to be the ideal hospital orderly, not having acquainted himself with basic domestic duties: 'nurses laughed at my efforts to wash floors'. What greater humiliation could there be for one so anxious to offer himself sacrificially to this great imperial cause? To make things worse, the thick fogs at Liverpool were blamed for heavy colds and influenza attacks that made his presence a constant threat to the health of patients.

Even the AIF, it began to appear, could offer no permanent solution to this young man's earnest desire to find his proper niche in life. He first tried outdoor work, then he was sent to the officers' mess to undertake the all-important role of washing dishes. He lasted long enough (one day in fact) to realise that the food was better in these select quarters than in those military circles in which he had moved. No Anzac could allow failure as a dishwasher to demoralise him. A call for men who could handle shorthand and typing offered Private Frank Jones other opportunities for service of the Empire. The office of the Senior Medical Officer at Darlinghurst required two suitably qualified clerks. A rapid attempt to learn Boyd Shorthand along with a couple of typing lessons provided sufficient qualifications to get Private Jones the office job he now sought. More than that, his new role allowed him to rise in status among those denominated 'other ranks'. He was now Lance Corporal Jones, and the superior in rank to his fellow appointee – described as 'a capable railway clerk'.

Alas, Lance Corporal Jones was not long to retain that one stripe on the arm of his military jacket. Despite (or perhaps because of) long nights spent at the typewriter, Lance Corporal Jones and his solitary subordinate were relieved of this avenue for service of the Empire after a fortnight. To add insult to injury, they were replaced by two girls. Thereafter Lance Corporal Jones would be assigned to messenger duties, but at least his evenings did not have to be spent bent over the typewriter, and there was ample leisure time for such intellectual pursuits as playing draughts.

At this point in Lance Corporal Jones' military career, disaster came very close to terminating his opportunities of service to Nation and Empire. It had been the normal practice for Australian Medical Corps members to spend twelve months in 'home' camp hospitals, before being assigned for service overseas. A high-ranking officer, apparently thinking that opportunities for noble sacrifice were deficient on the home front, decided that this situation was intolerable. Orders were therefore issued that all men who had served three months or more 'at home' were to be discharged. Lance Corporal Jones was beginning to reconcile himself to the awful fate of life as a civilian in wartime, when the troublesome orders were revoked and his opportunities for self-sacrifice were renewed.

On return to Liverpool Camp Frank Jones was stripped of his Lance Corporal's rank, and once more joined the swollen numbers of Australia's private soldiers. His only other opportunity to exert the doubtful authority of a Lance Corporal, was when he was again given that privileged status in order that he might properly exercise the solemn responsibility of dispensing contraceptives at the camp gate, to soldiers going on leave. His earlier duties at the army's venereal diseases hospital presumably made him a conscientious servant of the king, in this new role. The Lance Corporal's rank again disappeared when he was relieved of those prophylactic duties at the camp gate, and thereafter Frank Jones appears in the official records as 'private'. When he was later assigned to the Australian Light Horse, he was given the equivalent cavalryman's rank of 'trooper'.

Frank Jones in 1917

In February 1917, Private Jones became Trooper Jones, with the 1st Light Horse Field Ambulance. Opportunities for self-sacrifice appeared to be increasing as his unit boarded a small troop transport, the *S.S. Itria*, bound for Melbourne. At least Trooper Jones had succeeded in getting onto the ocean, two years after his initial attempt. The Light Horse reinforcements plus their horses duly arrived at Melbourne, only to hear that a German raider was prowling the high seas and that they would have to await a convoy escort before proceeding closer to the war zone. Initially the reinforcements were encamped near Melbourne, but it was soon decided to remove them some distance inland to the army's Seymour Camp. An outbreak of viral infections led to the tents at Seymour being pulled down all day, but with nothing to do it proved a carefree life.

A Warrior Abroad

The reinforcements for the Middle East did not again board ship until 10 May 1917, when the requisite escort vessels were available. The troops then set out for Egypt on the *S.S. Boorara*, which had enjoyed a prewar existence as a German cargo vessel in the Pacific trade before being commandeered by the Australian navy. The original steel decks were hardly suited to the large-scale carriage of troops across the equatorial zone, so a second layer of timber decking had been added. Highly obnoxious odours emanated from the bilge water between the two layers of decking, as the convoy of about a dozen ships set out intrepidly for the Great Australian Bight under the protective guns of a cruiser escort kindly supplied by the Imperial Japanese Navy. The long-retired Trooper Jones described that passage across the Bight as 'bobbing like corks', and the normal bouts of acute seasickness among long-term landlubbers

Aboard troop ship *S.S. Boorara*

provided the least of their worries. Storms tossed them hither and thither, while measles and mumps began to take serious toll on adult men. Worse than that, there were cases of meningitis aboard, requiring careful treatment. The 'terrible stench' from between decks did not decrease on the high seas, while Trooper Jones attended to a meningitis patient in the isolation hospital near the rear of the ship.

A successful passage of the Great Australian Bight did not put an end to the woes of those gallant reinforcements for the Australian Light Horse. Soon after departing the port of Fremantle, crewmen discovered that water supplies were contaminated. Supplies of alternative fluids (for 'other ranks' anyway) were limited to lemonade, and this disappeared rapidly forcing the troops back upon their impure water. Fortunately, the elements remained calm, allowing an easy sea passage to Colombo, where ample fresh water was available.

From Colombo, the *S.S. Boorara* bumped across to Africa, turning up the eastern coast of that continent bound for the Suez Canal. Disembarking at Suez, men and horses entrained in open rail trucks for Ismailia, and transferred thence to a base camp at Moascar. Contagious diseases had continued to plague the reinforcements. There was a period of enforced quarantine before any men could be sent on closer to the front line, where light-horsemen in association with British and other colonial troops confronted substantial Turkish forces. The Turkish were assisted by German military advisers, intent on harrying that vital British supply route, the Suez Canal.

Having eventually achieved his long-term objective of getting into a region where the serious business of military self-sacrifice might be made more of a reality than hitherto, Frank Jones was disgusted to find himself again relegated to the role of clerk. Against his will, Trooper Jones was assigned to the office of the Senior Medical Officer at Moascar Base Camp, Major Yuille. No great sacrifice about this role, which Frank Hackett-Jones much later described as 'a very comfortable job'. There was even a bed in the office. An assistant from Adelaide, of Quaker background, did much of what work there was to do. It appears that the busiest individual in that office was a chameleon that claimed dominion over the tabletop, which provided a convenient base from which to conduct its fly-catching operations.

Frank Jones had acquired a love of stylish horses from his Methodist minister father, long noted for possessing the smartest steeds in whichever country town he happened to be serving. In a pre-motor era, the style of one's horses had something of the status significance that the model of one's car has today. Major Yuille possessed two horses, and it was to be expected that a Major's horses should be a cut above those of the common trooper. Trooper Jones soon became friendly with the groom of the Major's horses, who happened to be a very popular novelist in Australia during the first quarter of this century: one Nat Gould. Gould was most noted for his racing stories, hence presumably his grooming role in the Middle East. Frank Jones and Nat Gould relieved the boredom of their military lives by conducting private horse races with the aid of the Major's speedy steeds. Opportunities for noble self-sacrifice were still being denied the young recruit from the Bureau of Statistics.

However, fate (aided a little by Trooper Jones) was soon to change that situation. During the preparations for a major military advance upon Beersheba, Major Yuille was assigned to a front-line posting, leaving one Major Burke Gaffney as Commanding Officer at Moascar. One of Trooper Jones' duties was to prepare the lists of reinforcements for service at the front, under his Commanding Officer's instructions. In the process of transition between the departure of Major Yuille and the effective takeover of responsibilities by Major Burke Gaffney, Trooper Jones used his 'power of the pen' to ensure that he was among the next batch of lucky troops bound for the front line, with its varied range of opportunities for heroic self-sacrifice. Major Burke Gaffney was informed on the authority of Trooper Jones that Major Yuille had arranged for the Quaker assistant to take over the important duties at Moascar Base Camp. Trooper Jones had at last succeeded in his struggle to overcome those serious physical defects of eyesight, and feet structure, that thwarted his martial and self-sacrificial instincts.

A light-horseman bound for spheres of urgent military activity required a trusty horse, and in Trooper Jones' case, preferably one that possessed a little style and spirit. At the remount depot a 'nice-looking black horse' caught the young soldier's eye, and he promptly claimed it as his own war-steed. Trooper Jones' judgement of horseflesh proved to be of a high order, but his choice of steed eventually proved highly embarrassing. As his Light Horse reinforcements group moved steadily closer to the front line, riding four abreast in troop, it became apparent that Trooper Jones' steed had been accustomed to carry officers of rank. Despite the young soldier's attempts at dissuasion it insisted on taking its rightful place at the head of the military contingent. This embarrassment was removed upon arrival at the Field Hospital, where a resident dentist (of considerably higher rank than Trooper Jones) initiated an exchange of horses, which the aspiring young soldier had to reluctantly facilitate.

Action with the Light Horse

Even upon arrival at the Field Hospital, close behind an Anzac front line in Palestine, life did not turn out to be immediately sacrificial. It was a quiet period, and Trooper Jones joined the stretcher bearers at filling in time with odd jobs. There was one hour's horse-picket duty each night, and on one occasion the 'old soldier' whose term of duty preceded that of Trooper Jones slept on so that our aspiring young warrior was not woken for his turn. Fortunately, no enemy force swept down upon the cavalry lines that night, and the AIF remained blissfully unaware of the dangers to which its unguarded steeds had been exposed.

Only a liberal supply of horses relieved the monotony of Trooper Jones' life behind the front lines at this time when all was quiet. It was his first opportunity to experience the Bedouin's horseback life in the desert for himself. On one uncomfortable occasion Trooper

Playing two-up

Trooper Frank Harold Jones in Palestine

Jones was afflicted by a sudden and acute attack of lumbago while on solitary desert patrol. Finding himself very alone, surrounded by nothing but miles of rolling sand and quite unable to mount his trusty steed, the young soldier began to see possibilities of self-sacrifice that were much more real than those he had previously perceived. However, at this perilous point in his military career, he was found by a British troop on desert patrol and promptly lifted back into the saddle. The desert was not to claim this eager young Anzac so readily.

In fact, in his next misadventure with a horse, it was to be the desert sands that saved Trooper Jones' life. On that occasion his noble steed, previously unacquainted with the sight and smell of camels, was so revolted by the sight of these bumpy beasts that it suddenly reared over upon its back, pinning the light-horseman in a deep sand drift. Having dislodged its jockey, the terrified steed headed off at speed towards the nearest watering place, leaving its stunned rider to shake of the clinging remains of that desert sand to which he owed his continuing opportunities for self-sacrifice to Nation and Empire.

Trooper Jones' first active involvement in the serious business of what the British Army knew as the Turkish Campaigns in Syria was as the driver of what was known as 'a limber wagon'. These desert ambulances were sometimes referred to as 'sand carts' because of their unusually wide steel tyres. The vehicle was drawn by four horses harnessed as two pairs, with one driver mounted upon the nearside horse of each pair. Trooper Jones' driver-assistant on his first venture into the ambulance business was a cheerful Egyptian named Ibrahim, described as a 'good chap'. At this point of his military career Frank was based near the port of Jaffa on what was then the Mediterranean coast of Syria. His first testing drive with a limber wagon took him from the Jewish settlement of Richon Le Zion (six miles south of Jaffa) to the inland town of Nablus, situated on a main north-south overland route some miles to the north-east.

There is no indication of what, if anything, the limber wagon carried on its circuitous travels. However, we do know that it proceeded from Nablus down the main road route to Jerusalem, and thence to the Jordan River's West Bank. At that time there were good reasons for preferring the West Bank, the East Bank having been occupied by two large items of German artillery lovingly known to the diggers as 'Jericho Jane' and 'Nablus Nellie'. Trooper Jones considered the daily bombardments from those long-range guns to be 'harmless', but they were his first experience of the real thing in the self-sacrifice business.

Things suddenly hotted up for the young light-horseman when his unit unexpectedly found itself part of the Front Line, and then behind the enemy lines, in late April 1918. A British raid planned by General Allenby upon the cities of Es Salt and Amman, well to the west of the Jordan River, went wrong for the British and their colonial helpers. Turkish resistance proved to be surprisingly strong, and the dedication of allied Arab forces not so reliable.

In the confused skirmishing that ensued, the 4th Light Horse Brigade was outflanked by Turkish units and the British artillery and Anzac ambulance lines were overrun, with part of the field ambulance unit being captured by the Turks. The first evidence that Trooper Jones had that his opportunities for self-sacrifice were greatly enhanced was when the Royal Horse Artillery retreated through the field ambulance station, having first destroyed its own lethal hardware.

The middle of 1918 was a significant turning point in the Syrian campaigns for those Australians and New Zealanders fighting there. At the end of April 1918 General Allenby had been forced to part with his 52nd and 74th divisions, ten British battalions drawn from other divisions in the area, nine regiments of yeomanry, five-and-a-half siege batteries and five machine-gun companies. These seasoned troops were required for more vital service in the French offensives of 1918. In return, General Allenby received the 3rd (Lahore) and 7th (Meerut) divisions of the Indian Army via Mesopotamia, and Indian cavalry released from France. Although the main Indian contingents were seasoned troops, the reinforcements that were sent in to maintain their numbers were untried and less reliable men. The raids on Es Salt and Amman were part of a diversionary tactic to distract Turkish attention from Allenby's predicament in having to rearrange his much disrupted forces, and also to make the Turks think (falsely) that the British were preparing to direct their major assault towards Damascus via Gilead. Fortunately Trooper Jones was not among those men of the Light Horse Ambulance who were captured by the Turks during Allenby's diversionary raids, or his opportunities for self-sacrifice would have been severely restricted.[9]

Although Allenby had lost many of the seasoned troops in whom he felt confidence to the French campaigns, other factors were turning in his favour. The German Taubes (fast and silent war planes by the standards of that day) had previously dominated the Syrian skies, but British planes were about to gain superiority in the air. The disappearance of the German planes meant that the Turkish armies were deprived of much of the information on troop movements to which they had become accustomed, and Allenby's troops were no longer to be frustrated by German bombing raids on their supply lines.

First Light Horse Field Ambulance

First Light Horse Field Ambulance

Frank, seated, with friends

The Light Mule Field Ambulance? Frank, second from top left, with friends and local guides

Meanwhile, Trooper Jones spent a very unpleasant 1918 summer season in the Jordan Valley. The oppressive summer climate was considered suitable only for the presence of Australians and Indians, and the official history volume on the Australians at war in the Middle East has described a horror scene of heat, dust, and nasty insects. In his latter years, Frank Hackett-Jones did not remember a situation as bad as that depicted by the official war historian Henry Gullett, but it certainly had been unpleasant.

Trooper Jones applied to join a field dressing station with one of the three regiments that made up his brigade of Light Horse Ambulance. He was, however, sent to the first vacancy that occurred, which was with the Anzac Divisional Train of the Army Service Corps. His job was to convey food, ammunition, and other essential military supplies to the troops at the front. As previously, each Australian driver had an Egyptian assistant driver, but these more heavily laden vehicles were usually drawn by five horses or by five mules.

Soon thereafter Frank Jones found himself once more in control of a limber wagon ambulance, and part of a happy team of Anzacs. His section was headed by Sergeant Maurice Evans, a Gallipoli veteran, and Corporal David Horne who had been a schoolteacher. The other trooper on the four-man ambulance team was Bert Hudson, a former Sydney clerk with whom Frank Jones would long maintain associations. All the others were more experienced in the needs of military medicine than was Trooper Jones, his only training to that point having been in the treatment of venereal diseases. Most of his current Syrian experience related to treating and bandaging septic sores, the results of serious dietary deficiencies endured by the Australian troops.

If opportunities for self-sacrifice still appeared limited, there were chances to pursue other long-term educational interests. Although he had long since given up any ideas of becoming a professional archaeologist, the lure of the Holy Land and its ancient monuments was still strong. The lower Jordan Valley in the vicinity of Jericho was rich in biblical allusions. When he found himself based near the foot of the Mount of Temptation, biblical associations were obvious. Close by was the Wady Kelt, and he (wrongly) believed that this stream was the 'brook' associated with a popular Old Testament story concerning the prophet Elijah. The ruins of a Greek monastery adorned the mount itself, on a site hollowed out of the mountainside. The young light-horseman would sometimes climb to the monastery to enjoy its swimming pool. He also explored the rugged countryside of Brech Cherith, where there was another Greek monastery.

The ambulance unit was encamped upon a plain of loose stones, home to innumerable scorpions. Troops suffering from

Frank Hackett-Jones in the Jordan Valley ...

... with a goddess ...

... and with a temple guide

scorpion bites were treated as for snakebite at home, by lance, tourniquet and whisky. It is unclear whether the whisky was administered orally or intravenously. Presumably any digger would have considered the latter procedure a waste of good whisky. A long and sometimes highly uncomfortable summer was completely spent in that historic Jordan Valley, with a few days off to inspect Bethlehem.[10]

The British army's strategy for its later 1918 campaign in Syria was working effectively. Allenby had bluffed the Turks into believing that his aim was to take Amman and areas to the east of Jordan, whereas he was preparing for a powerful coastal offensive. Dummy camps and dummy horse lines were spread over a wide area, and horses sweated freely as wagons were used to maximum effect in throwing up clouds of dust. With the German air force now barred from close observation of the real situation, the main Turkish force was kept to the East of the Jordan, whereas the coastal strip was left relatively lightly defended. A small force of Anzacs assisted by untried Indian and West Indian reinforcements was all that the Turks in fact faced in what they believed to be their problem sector.

When the British coastal offensive began, Trooper Frank Jones was attached to the New Zealand section of the Anzac Divisional Train. In September 1918, Allenby's British forces moved suddenly. While his mounted troops encircled the Turkish rear, causing a rout, British planes bombed key railway targets and Arab allies occupied the important Deraa rail junction. With their supply lines cut, the Turkish forces were soon in full retreat, with panic leading to further disasters. Many Turkish prisoners surrendered to the Anzacs, the Turks being fearful for their lives should they fall into the hands of vengeful Arabs. British control of the skies meant that dismembered divisions of retreating Turks from west of Jordan were easily picked up by British or Anzac units, before they could join up with intact Turkish armies to the east.[11]

Disease, Demoralisation and Demobilisation

Frank Jones became caught up in the push of the victorious British forces towards Amman in the east. The New Zealand Mounted Rifles with whom he then worked were operating in malarial country, and suffering extremely heavy losses of manpower through disease. One tenth of the men in the entire Divisional Train were being evacuated each day, suffering from malaria. Trooper Jones was himself soon afflicted, and sent to a field hospital suffering from a high fever. He would long remember hospital meals that consisted of two boiled eggs. Transferred from one field hospital to another, he eventually found himself in the 31st General Hospital at Cairo in Egypt. After two weeks in bed he was granted a week's leave, and seized the opportunity to visit the fascinating and historic ruins of ancient Luxor on the Nile. This trip occurred several years before his archaeologically oriented favourite uncle, James Thompson Hackett, died at the site of that ancient Egyptian imperial centre.

Early in November of 1918, Trooper F.H. Jones returned to the Anzac Divisional Train in Syria. The ashes of Surafend were still smouldering after a colonial onslaught upon that centre, but an armistice had been signed with Turkey. The Germans had broken through the British lines in France earlier that year, and there had been calls to send the Light Horse to Europe. When the first news came through that the Germans had also capitulated, Trooper Jones and his Anzac friends greeted the reports with polite scepticism: 'we were far from thinking the war was over'. When it was confirmed that an armistice had been signed in Europe on 11 November 1918, the troops felt a quiet satisfaction along with their surprise. The end had come very suddenly in the Middle East, and the light-horsemen were even more surprised to find that the Germans, who had so recently caused many crack British units to be hurriedly called back from Syria, had collapsed in the European theatre of the war. The opportunities for glorious sacrifice had passed, but Trooper Jones could rest comfortably in the knowledge that he had eventually taken part (as a medical assistant) in serious military action, and had himself fallen a victim to malaria in the cause for which he had been so keen to fight, against considerable personal odds.[12]

Trooper Jones' Middle Eastern war experiences were to end on a low note, which he always felt that he could have done without. He was attached to a group of Australians and New Zealanders who were encamped near the recently 'liberated' Arab settlement of Surafend. In a not uncommon incident of Middle Eastern military experience, a party of local Arabs had been interrupted while engaged in a nocturnal thieving expedition at the camp. When the Anzacs gave chase, a New Zealand sergeant was shot dead by the retreating marauders. Irate New Zealanders backed by Australians and some British troops demanded that the village hand over the culprits for appropriate punishment. When this demand was rejected, a party of Anzacs (allegedly supported by British artillery men wielding knotted-steel trace-chains) executed their own rough justice upon the men of Surafend.

That unfortunate incident at Surafend was used by H.W. Gullett to bring to a conclusion his official World War I history of the Australian campaigns in the Middle East. It represented a common theme of that era, when Anzac troops frequently came into open conflict with British military officers because of the broad gulf that existed between their conceptions of what represented 'a fair go' in martial matters. Many years later Dame Mabel Brooks, who had been an Australian war nurse at the time, also used the Surafend incident in the concluding section of her book of memoirs entitled *Riders of Time*:

> Now they were going home; and to them the loss of a comrade, at this late stage, by murder at the hands of a race they despised, called for instant justice; nevertheless the disciplinary branch of General Headquarters still continued in its studied omission to punish Arabs for crimes of violence ... They grimly passed out all the women and children from the village; and with heavy staves fell on the men and set fire to the hovels. Some Arabs were killed and some escaped without injury and the flames lit the countryside. It is said British Artillery also moved in, knotting their trace-chains as weapons ...[13]

With the war officially ended, this application of 'lynch law' was highly embarrassing to British authorities, and General Allenby expressed great indignation at the assault upon 'Arab friends'. The Anzac division was drawn up in hollow formation, while Allenby thundered: 'Men of this glorious Anzac Division, I was proud of you once, I am proud of you no longer. There are murderers in front of me ...' Trooper Frank Jones was not present on this memorable occasion. He hated all sorts of parades, and had volunteered for medical-tent duty. The Anzacs saw injustice and irony in the fact that British troops who had played a significant role in the raid on Surafend were placed behind the general, while he upbraided the men from the Antipodes.

Quarantine at Sydney's North Head

It obviously suited British diplomatic purposes that blame for the incident should be placed upon 'undisciplined colonial troops', and unquestionably New Zealanders had initiated the act of retribution. Trooper Jones shared in the general 'punishment' of the Anzacs. He was sent back to a camp at Rafa, surrounded by sand and boredom, to await repatriation to Australia and ultimate discharge from the AIF.

The war was over, and Trooper Jones' considerable initiative was applied to the problem of getting home as soon as possible from what had ended as a not-so-glorious military adventure. Learning that university students were obtaining preference in being shipped home, Trooper Jones again listed himself as a Sydney University student for the occasion. Once home, it would be easy to avoid university studies from his secure Bureau of Statistics job base.

Trooper Frank Jones duly embarked on the *S.S. Port Sydney* in April 1919, and relieved the boredom of the long trip home by giving lectures on bookkeeping to a small class. There were less enjoyable chores like washing hospital blankets, but badly soiled items could be tossed out of a convenient porthole. The *Port Sydney* arrived at its home port in the midst of the serious Spanish Influenza epidemic that contributed to so many Australian deaths in 1919. Returning troops were quarantined for a fortnight at North Head, before being let loose upon the civilian world. Trooper Frank Harold Jones received his discharge certificate on 27 June 1919 and was relieved that the Surafend incident had not damaged his military record too seriously: he was discharged from the AIF as medically unfit, not due to misconduct.[14]

CHAPTER 5

AN ASPIRING PUBLIC SERVANT:
THE 1920s

Frank Harold Jones reappeared on the New South Wales Public Service Lists for 1919, restored to the same status as he had held prior to military enlistment in 1916 – that of a clerk in the clerical division of the Bureau of Statistics. It was identical to the position allotted to him on 1 September 1913, and his annual salary of £195 (slightly below the average Sydney wage in 1920) reflected a lowly status. However, change was afoot in the Bureau of Statistics, which was to be to the advantage of Frank Jones. In June 1919 the *New South Wales Government Gazette* announced the appointment of Horace Alexander Smith, previously Chief Assistant at the Bureau of Statistics, as the new Government Statistician, Registrar and Actuary of Friendly Societies and Trade Unions.[1]

The return to Sydney and family

Inspector of Friendly Societies

Later in that year a major reconstruction of the Bureau took place, involving several promotions and changes of job designation. Thomas Waites, who had been Frank Jones' immediate boss prior to his period of war service, became Chief Assistant in the Bureau. Bertie P. McEvoy was promoted to Waites' previous office of Chief Clerk in the Friendly Societies Branch. With the promotion to higher duties of the previous Inspector of Friendly Societies, that position was divided into two parts. Henry W. Whealey became the Senior Inspector of Friendly Societies from 1 July 1919, while Frank H. Jones was promoted to the newly created position of Junior Inspector of Friendly Societies. This was a major break for the young public servant, who had kicked himself clear of the general run of clerks, and salary rises quickly lifted him out of the financial rut in which he had previously been bogged down. Initially, the Junior Inspector's appointment only lifted his annual salary to a modest £225, at a time when the basic wage amounted to £156 per year. However, this was transformed by 1920 into the healthier figure of £294, and by 1921 Frank Jones had attained to a salary of £315 in the Bureau of Statistics.[2]

On returning from war service, Frank Jones' mind had immediately returned to earlier attempts to gain accountancy qualifications, to further enhance career opportunities. He called on his old accountancy coach, and learned that the final examinations in accounting and auditing were scheduled for September 1919. Frank's coach advised him to have a go. At the ensuing examinations, something of Frank Jones' pre-university self-confidence was restored when he topped the State of New South Wales in Accountancy examinations, and was awarded a gold medal. The gold medal partly explains his relatively rapid salary rises from that point in time. As he said many decades later, the gold medal for Accountancy was 'very useful' in pay tussles with the Public Service Board. In 1920 Frank Jones completed his formal Accountancy qualifications by passing in the final law subject required. He was then made an associate in what later became known as the Society of Accountants of Australia.

By 1920 Frank's parents had moved from their North Parramatta farmlet to a more obviously outer-suburban address at Harris Park, just on the Sydney side of Parramatta. He was now only two minutes walk from Harris Park railway station, on a major suburban train route. This was also to be Frank Jones' motorcycle phase. He was the proud possessor of a prewar Bradbury machine, whose two-cylinder motor was claimed to produce six horsepower at full rattle. Local roads were rough, which encouraged more or less important pieces of the machine to come free periodically, and the motorcycle was largely used for going to golf.

Henceforth Frank Jones' earlier sporting interests were to be abandoned in favour of the golf course, as befitted an aspiring public servant. He became an enthusiastic member of the Parramatta Golf Club, taking golf lessons from any 'professional' who happened to be within convenient proximity. Saturday came to have a special importance in Frank's life. He was at the Sydney office from 9 a.m. until midday, and took a brief lunch break around 1 p.m. in order to be on a train headed for Parramatta and golf by 1:20 p.m.[3]

We know little of what Frank Jones actually achieved at the Bureau of Statistics in these years of the early 1920s. Presumably, his Accountancy qualifications were useful in the checking of books and periodic balance sheets from the many friendly societies scattered around New South Wales. The amazing range of friendly societies then registered in New South

Wales is indicated by the massive and well-thumbed indexes still held by the New South Wales Government Archives at Kingswood. Doubtless, these big indexes were well known to the young Frank Jones in his daily work.

One large index volume to the Friendly Societies Register relates to an earlier period: 1900 to 1910. It provides an interesting overview of the coming and going of such societies early this century. At the beginning of the century, with Australian federation in the air, the Australian Natives Association had branches all over New South Wales. However, the great majority of those local branches had disappeared prior to 1907, with branches at Broken Hill, South Broken Hill, Newcastle, and Deniliquin being among the few survivors.[4]

Friendly societies associated with various major religious denominations, especially the Catholic Church, continued strongly into the World War I period. There was the Australasian Holy Catholic Guild of St Mary and St Joseph Friendly Benefit Society, possessing lengthy lists of branches endowed with such names as Our Lady of Dolors Branch (Chatswood). Equally impressive were the pages and pages of branch names relating to the Hibernian-Australasian Catholic Benefit Society. Most branches took their names from favourite saints. There was St Mary's at West Wyalong, St Joseph's at Junee, St Patrick's at Ganmain, St Brigid's at Dubbo, and St Carthage's at Lismore, not to mention the occasional Star of the Sea or Sacred Heart branch. Not unrelated, though less obviously religious in name, was the Irish National Foresters' Friendly Society. This much smaller organisation included a St Mary's Cathedral Branch in Sydney, a Hope of Erin (female) branch at Broken Hill, an Owen Roe O'Neill branch at Glebe, and even a William E. Gladstone branch at Lithgow. This latter intrusion of a prominent English Protestant name reflects Gladstone's efforts to obtain home rule for Ireland, during the later 19th century.

At the other end of the local religious spectrum with which the young Frank Jones had to deal as Inspector of Friendly Societies, were such bodies as the Protestant Alliance Friendly Society of Australasia, Grand Council of New South Wales. Branch names tended to be of a different order to those of Catholic counterparts. Not surprisingly, no saints here. There was a Prince of Wales Lodge, a Cromwell Lodge, a John Knox Lodge, a Queen Victoria Lodge, a Lord Nelson Lodge, a Prince of Orange Lodge, and even a Garibaldi Lodge. Captain Cook gave his name to another lodge, and there was the occasional regional title as in Star of Cootamundra Lodge.

Even less respected by those Irish who enjoyed a drop of alcohol was the Independent Order of Rechabites, Salford Unity Friendly Society. This popular friendly society took up many pages of the registry index. Its long lists of branch names included a Perseverance Tent, a Press Forward Tent, an Onward and Upward Tent, a Haste to the Rescue Tent, a Nil Desperandum Tent, a Hurstville Lifeboat Tent, and even a Hope of Redfern Tent. No less formidable to patrons of Sydney public houses were the members of the Order of the Sons and Daughters of Temperance. This body was also going strong around the period of World War I. Branch names for this body included a British Lion Division, a Band Of Hope Division, a We Hope to Prosper Division, and a Happy Home Division.

Then there were the many lodges of a Masonic type. The Ancient Order of Foresters' Friendly Society of New South Wales was arranged by regional districts such as Sydney District, New England District, and Western District. Each district had its lists of town-based 'courts'. For example there was the court Pride of Mudgee, the court General Gordon, and the court Star of the Hunter. Frank Jones would also have had to be familiar with the many branches of the Grand United Order of Oddfellows Friendly Society of New South Wales, also organised by districts. The Pride of Waterloo, the Loyal Balmain, and the Glebe Union branches doubtless contrasted in membership to branches such as the Loyal Star of Bourke, or the Star of the West. There was also the Grand United Order of Free Gardeners of Australasia, with its Waratah Lodge, its White Rose Lodge, its Cornstalk Lodge, its Acorn Juvenile Lodge, its Passion Flower Lodge, and even its Sturt Pea Lodge.

Among the largest of these friendly societies was the Manchester Unity Independent Order of Oddfellows Friendly Society in New South Wales. Branches of this body were also arranged by region, and the Tweed River District boasted such members as the Loyal Tumbulgum Lodge at Tumbulgum, and the Loyal Tweed Lodge at Murwillumbah. The United Ancient Order of Druids Friendly Society also doubtless took up many hours of the time of the young Inspector of Friendly Societies at the Bureau of Statistics. As one would expect, the oak tree came to the fore in branch naming efforts. There was a Royal Oak Lodge, a Heart of Oak Lodge, a Rylstone Oak Lodge, and a Silver Oak Lodge, and there was even a Boadicea Lodge and a Prince Alfred Lodge.

When the Junior Inspector of Friendly Societies had familiarised himself with the financial mysteries pertaining to such major friendly societies, there would be a host of minor bodies upon which to keep an eye. There was, for instance, The Coloured Progressive Association of the British Empire, registered in April 1904. Just how that body related to a White Australia policy is unclear to this author. Then there were various scattered Dispensary groups, like the Balmain United Friendly Societies Dispensary founded in 1902, and the Burwood District Friendly Societies Dispensary set up in 1908. An occasional society designed to protect members against the expenses related to industrial accident can be found. The Cape Hawke Sawmill Employees' Accident Society, first registered in August 1908, presumably protected its members against very real risks.

There were many other such minor bodies to whose books and balance sheets Frank Jones would have had to pay attention at some time after 1913. These included the Teachers' Mutual Assurance Association of New South Wales, the Trolly Draymen and Carters' Accident Insurance Society, the New South Wales Tramway Employees' Association, the New South Wales Harbours and Rivers Provident Fund, and the New South Wales Naval Brigade Widows' and Orphans' Provident Society. Perhaps we ought not to be surprised that by 1922 the Junior Inspector of Friendly Societies was again looking for a change of employment. He was even prepared to take a position that meant reverting to the humble title of clerk in the New South Wales Public Service. The Public Service Lists for 1923 indicate that Frank H. Jones was appointed to the position of clerk in the Lands Department, Returned Soldiers' Settlement Branch, on 5 May 1922.[5]

With the Returned Soldier Settlers Scheme

At about that time Frank Jones also worked on the gathering of information for two New South Wales Royal Commissions. These were the Necessary Commodities Commission which was designed to restrict profiteering, and the Randwick Railway Workshops Commission which was set up to investigate a strike situation and union claims of increased efficiency. Between April 1920 and July 1922, New South Wales was governed by Labor administrations, initially led by John Storey and more latterly by James Dooley. The one-time boiler-maker-turned-premier John Storey had brought much invective upon his head both in New South Wales and in London during 1921, by plans to resume large New South Wales pastoral properties for closer settlement. Many such large properties were owned by English interests, and Storey's move was at first widely understood in England as a socialist 'grab'.[6]

The State political situation changed on 7 July 1922, with the accession of a coalition of Nationalists and Progressives under G.W. Fuller. This government retained power until June 1925, so that it was a convenient time for Frank Jones to be moving his employment to an obvious rural-interest area like the Lands Department. These years between mid-1922 and mid-1925 provided the only extensive period of conservative government that Frank Jones would experience as a New South Wales public servant. Walter E. Wearne was Secretary for Lands and Minister for Forests in that Fuller coalition ministry. Perhaps the most famous (or infamous) of that ministerial team was its Minister for Justice, T.J. Ley, who became notorious in England at a later date when he was connected with a widely publicised and gory murder case. He was later admitted to an institution for the criminally insane.[7]

That period in the middle of 1922 when Frank Jones transferred across to the Returned Soldiers' Settlement Branch of the Lands Department appears to have been one of considerable build-up in that branch. The *Government Gazette* indicates that a rash of male junior clerks and female shorthand-writers and typists moved in at virtually the same time. At the time Frank Jones arrived on the scene, Miss Camillius Maria Philomene Naughton and Miss Doris Edna Rourke would have been beginning to accustom themselves to the office furniture and personalities. We have no record of what he thought of them, or they of him. On 1 June 1922, at least three new male junior clerks also arrived to find places in the office system. More significantly, on the same day in May that F.H. Jones first appeared at this Lands Department office, one William Sydney Collier, Accountant from Griffith (previously with the Water Conservation and Irrigation Commission) arrived to take up the post of Acting Sub-Accountant with the Returned Soldiers' Settlement Branch.[8]

Many years later Frank Hackett-Jones reminisced that W.S. Collier had (in his previous role with the Irrigation Commission) been the senior of his new boss at the Returned Soldiers' Settlement Branch, the chief accountant L.W.G. Baker. For that reason Baker 'got little work out of him'. When the new team moved in during the middle of 1922 they found a very confused situation. The previous accountant had walked out of the job; the books were in such a hopeless muddle that it was impossible for anyone to do a proper job of accounting with them. The arrival of the very capable L.W.G. Baker to take charge of the branch's accounting improved things greatly. Frank Jones was next in line of 'accounting authority' to Baker and Collier, but because of Collier's tardiness the younger man received more of the work than he thought fair.[9]

The elderly Frank Hackett-Jones still thought of the Returned Soldiers' Settlement programme of the early 1920s as a very laudable scheme for providing government farm advances to allow returned soldiers to become established on their own farms. However, like similar plans in other states, the New South Wales scheme was afflicted by major defects. The land holdings were often too small to provide economic family-living units, and many applicants for blocks were men rendered unfit for heavy manual work by wartime injuries or maladies. It was not uncommon for applicants to lack any prior experience of life on the land. Such men, finding it difficult to hold down a regular job, were very likely to look for an escape to an imagined rural paradise where they could work at their own pace with no boss looking over their shoulder.

Various Closer Settlement Acts, including that of 1901, had encouraged closer settlement of New South Wales'"wide open spaces". Under this legislation land-holdings could be bought by State governments, and reallotted for more intensive small-farming uses. Provisions for compulsory government acquisition of land holdings were made under a revised Closer Settlement Act of 1904. In 1916, the Returned Soldiers Settlement Act was passed, and this enabled the allocation of sections of Crown land (or lands acquired under the provisions of the Closer Settlement Acts) for use as small farms by returned soldiers.

A classification committee was set up to investigate the qualifications of returned-soldier applicants for blocks under the scheme, and certificates were provided to men considered eligible. The 'qualification' usually related directly to the nature of their war service, rather than to other relevant factors like farming experience. The basic qualification was that applicants must have served overseas, have received a discharge other than for misconduct, and must still reside within the Commonwealth. In 1917 provision was made for schemes of group purchase by returned soldiers. The original Act of 1916 received continual minor amendments, those of 1917, 1919, 1922, 1924, and 1925 being relevant to Frank Jones' period of service in the Lands Department.[10]

Not all those returned soldiers who had been promised their old jobs back on return from the war were as lucky as Frank Jones in finding the promise made good,'but farms for heroes was an acceptable variant to governments eager to promote closer settlement'. The Commonwealth Government, being the authority constitutionally endowed with responsibility for national defence matters, had early taken an interest in the question of returning soldiers onto the land at war's end. As early as 1915, a Federal Parliamentary War Committee had accepted the responsibility of finding employment for returning soldiers. Results of a questionnaire submitted to Australian troops during 1916 indicated that about one quarter of them looked forward to a postwar life on the land. Of these, approximately half had no experience of farming, and only a small percentage possessed any capital to contribute to the enterprise.[11]

Between 1916 and 1918, while the New South Wales Returned Soldiers' Settlement Act was being planned, representatives of Commonwealth and States had agreed upon a major programme of placing ex-soldiers on the land. The Commonwealth's role would be to provide loan funds at very reasonable interest rates, and to provide soldier-settlers with basic sustenance funds until their properties became economic. The States would supply areas of lightly populated pastoral land, and it was envisaged that this land would carry intensively cultivated small farms for pigs and poultry, or orchards, vineyards, and market gardens. Even those returned soldiers who had the experience, the quality of soil, and the capital equipment to exploit that soil, would be confronted by a paucity of markets for their produce during the 1920s and 1930s.

Commonwealth and States formulated various soldier-settlement schemes within the context of that British imperial vision under the influence of which Australia had recruited its sons for service in Europe after 1914. Australia was to be the provider of food, raw materials, and a market for an industrialised motherland. However, British markets for the produce of Australian soldier-settlement blocks never matched the rosy dreams of the early 1920s. It had also long been believed by many eminent Australians that life in the country was morally superior to urban existence. Many civic leaders were alarmed by the movement of large numbers of people from rural areas, into what already seemed to be dangerously overcrowded cities.

The misery that ensued for many optimistic New South Wales soldier-settlers of the early 1920s is vividly illustrated by John Ritchie's account of those who took up blocks in the Macquarie Vale area, just outside of Bathurst. This varied settlement appeared to provide a wide range of opportunities for keen returned soldiers. There were orchard blocks, market-garden blocks, and one dairy farm of sixty acres. However, the Commonwealth sustenance money was a pittance of £2 per week for a married man, at a time when the basic wage was £3-17-0. Presumably, it was assumed that settlers could live off the produce of their own land. The maximum sustenance period was set at five years for an orchardist, and at only one year for a market gardener. By 1923 it was obvious that there would be no appreciable crops of fruit before the trees had reached eight years of age, and most settlers had quietly disappeared from their blocks in search of decent jobs. In 1926 five determined settlers remained at Macquarie Vale, and at Depression's end that number had dwindled to two. Those two hard-working and long-suffering men, neither having children to feed and clothe, could hardly be described as success stories.[12]

As one who had to oversee the accounts for what turned out to be a disastrous New South Wales soldier-settlement scheme, Frank Jones saw plenty of evidence of human misery. The pettiness of the official mind when it came to financial matters relating to the settlements is well evidenced by a collection of circulars produced by the scheme's directors between 1918 and 1924, and preserved in the New South Wales State Archives at Kingswood. In August 1924 the *Government Gazette* indicated that, at the end of the previous June, another periodic shake-up had occurred in Frank Jones' working environment. Long lists were printed of staff members who on 1 July were transferred from the Returned Soldiers' Settlement Branch to the Accounts Branch of the Lands Department. Frank Harold Jones' name was there, but there was only one female name to go with the twenty male clerks listed. To be sure, there were several shorthand writers and typists of the fairer sex in those lists.[13]

Decades later, Frank Hackett-Jones recalled that his previous accountant bosses, Baker and Collier, were then transferred to the Auditor General's Department leaving their youthful junior colleague to handle the joyless accounts relating to a soldier-settlement scheme that was by that time in big trouble. However, there were compensations for the young public servant. He was still without any domestic responsibilities, and living at the parental home near Parramatta. The 1924 Public Service Lists indicate that his salary had crept up to be over £444 – not bad for an unencumbered young man at that time. Certainly, he would have been the envy of any of those returned soldier-settlers whose tangled financial affairs he attempted to make sense of at the office each day.

While Frank Jones was in charge of Returned Soldiers' Settlement Accounts at the Lands Department in 1925, two events of some consequence occurred. One was the accession to political power in New South Wales of Labor Premier J.T. Lang, the real-estate agent at Auburn when Frank Jones was undertaking his brief teaching spell at Auburn's primary school in 1913. Labor was in power in New South Wales from June 1925, and everybody soon knew it. The other event was more personal, but every bit as memorable. The Minutes of the New South Wales Methodist Conference for 1925 printed an obituary for Rev. Charles Jones, who had been an active minister of that Church for about 57 years and had died on 12 February 1925.

The eulogy was very flattering (measured by Methodist values) to Frank Jones' father.

> He put first things first, he insisted on the fundamentals, he preached and laboured for individual conversions, and rejoiced in nothing more than the winning of souls to allegiance to God. He had a fine scorn for conventions, and was fearless and uncompromising in his criticism of the facts of life about him. He never courted popularity, but his steadfast sincerity won the respect of the communities where he toiled. He was always loyal, at every cost, to any line of conduct that conscience told him was right. He was a preacher of evangelical fervour; an original thinker, who applied his faith to the practical things of daily life.

In addition to all that, he was described as a tender-hearted pastor of the grief-stricken, and a meticulous and careful church administrator. Even allowing for the exaggerations of an ecclesiastical obituary, the parental role model for young Frank Jones was a formidable one. Rev. Charles Jones' portrait is still rather awe-inspiring. The young Frank Jones must have lived in the shadow of this awesome parent for many years. He appears sometimes to have known pangs of guilt, that he was not built to be such a powerful 'servant of the Lord'.[14]

A lengthy obituary oration was printed in *The Methodist*, and attributed to Charles Jones' long-time friend and ministerial colleague, Dr Carruthers. A more human picture is there presented of the recently departed minister:

> He was in a sense a unique man. He had his own methods; he copied no man, and it would not have been wise for any man to attempt to copy him. Sometimes apparently brusque; always straight and outspoken, he yet carried within him a tender heart and a soul concerned for the spiritual welfare of his people. He had his tastes and foibles – who has not? He loved a good horse, and was never without one from the day he entered the ministry ... He was ever diligent – never idle or unemployed He was not always understood. He never studied the arts of finesse, or sought to curry favour ... Some people thought him a rough diamond; but if the edges were not always smooth the quality was there and he was a diamond ... An old-time Methodist, with little or no time for new views of the Bible or new methods in evangelism. He believed in the old truths.[15]

Rev. Charles Jones' death brought a spate of letters of sympathy from a wide range of friends and associates, both within and without the Methodist community. One letter came from E.K. Bowden on House of Representatives letterhead, indicating his respect for the dead man. Another came to Frank Jones on New South Wales Treasury letterhead, expressing the condolences of his one-time boss at the Lands Department. There was another letter to Frank Jones from his associates at the Parramatta Golf Club, and numerous letters of condolence to his mother from eminent Methodist ministers.[16]

The Inspector of Co-operative Societies

As from 27 January 1926, Frank Harold Jones was back among his old associates at the Bureau of Statistics. However, he was no longer in the section dealing specifically with friendly societies and their interminable statistics. His new title of office was Junior Inspector of Co-operative

Societies. A few things had changed at the Bureau while he had been dealing with the financial miseries of returned soldiers who had gone onto the land. In November 1925, less than two months prior to Frank Jones' return to the Bureau, Thomas Waites, who had been his first public service boss in 1913 (at that time Chief Clerk in the friendly societies' section), became the new Government Statistician, Registrar of Co-operative Societies and Registrar of Friendly Societies and Trade Unions. At the same time, Frank's other long-time associate at the Bureau, Bertie P. McEvoy, became Waites' deputy as Chief Assistant.

However, not all of F.H. Jones' previous superiors in the system were still rated above him. By sidestepping into the Lands Department for a few years, Frank had managed to pass the salary scale of Henry W. Whealey, the man who had been Senior Inspector of Friendly Societies in 1921 when Frank had the lowlier role (and pay) associated with being his Junior Inspector. By 1927-28 there was only one Registrar of Friendly Societies, still Whealey, but his salary was beginning to drop significantly behind that of F.H. Jones, recently returned as the Bureau's second Inspector of Co-operative Societies. Although age usually meant promotion in the public service, it had not done so for Whealey. Born early in 1865, he was very much Frank Jones' senior in the service, having entered it in May 1881. Whealey had known no promotion since July 1919. It appears that the role of friendly societies in New South Wales life (in which Whealey specialised) was diminishing markedly, at a time when the role of co-operatives was being encouraged by State governments. The much younger F.H. Jones had managed to get with the action by his detour through the Lands Department, but perhaps his longstanding good relationship with Thomas Waites at the Bureau of Statistics assisted that situation.

J.T. Lang's Labor administrations in New South Wales encouraged the co-operative movement generally, and the government registered a new series of co-operative bodies at that time which included building societies, retail stores, and fruit growers' packing houses. Lang had been involved in selling houses and property from the turn of the century, and despite his 'slum hero' image had become a reasonably wealthy man on the basis of those real-estate dealings. As early as 1906 he had been deeply involved as secretary with the local Starr-Bowkett Co-operative Building Society at Auburn, then on the developing western fringe of Sydney. Because of his background, Lang especially encouraged building societies as a part-answer to those acute problems of housing in Sydney with which he had long been familiar.

Labor administrations on either side of World War I had attempted a more direct governmental attack on the acute housing problems of lowly-paid working class families in Sydney. In 1912 an idealistic New South Wales Labor Government had planned the Daceyville Settlement, on a British 'garden city' model that had been implemented at Letchworth and Hampstead in Greater London. J. C. Dacey, Colonial Treasurer at the time, was the first chairman of a New South Wales Housing Board that supervised such schemes. One knowledgeable modern commentator on that prewar Daceyville Settlement scheme obviously regards it as a novel success story among government attempts to overcome Sydney housing problems. Peter Spearritt has commented on Daceyville's charming wood and brick bungalows, later condemned to sit 'amidst the worst excesses of the sixties flat boom'. In 1917 a similar 'garden suburb' scheme was implemented for returning soldiers, on the waste sandhills of Matraville, behind Daceyville. Even in 1918, the Daceyville project was far from being completed, and demand was escalating with 353 applicants for 20 rental cottages in 1919. The Labor-inspired New South Wales Housing Board, although not achieving much of what had been hoped from it, constructed much-needed houses at Bunnerong, Gladesville, and at Stockton in Newcastle. It also acted as a source of housing finance, through New South Wales' State Savings Bank, to 516 aspiring home owners.[17]

That New South Wales Housing Board was disbanded by the incoming Fuller Nationalist Government in 1924, allegedly because of a faulty administration and its inability to pay its own way from public-housing rentals. With Labor's return to power in New South Wales under Jack Lang in 1925, the emphasis would be more on government assistance in the provision of finance to assist private home ownership. The public-rental-housing problem had proved 'too hard' for previous Labor administrators, and whatever his professed sympathies with the underprivileged, Lang's life experience related more to those who could afford to buy or sell a house of their own. Frank Jones' experiences as Inspector of Co-operative Societies while Jack Lang ruled from Sydney would prove useful to him in the darker days of World War II, when he would become the foundation Legal Officer to the newly-formed Housing Commission of New South Wales.[18]

Between 1926 and 1928 the aspiring young public servant travelled widely around New South Wales, checking the records and accounts of co-operative societies, and conducting spot checks to ensure that all was well. The Bureau of Statistics had been transferred from its previous home in the Chief Secretary's Department, into the fold of the Colonial Treasurer's Department. During the years 1926-1927, this meant that for some time Frank Jones operated in a section of the New South Wales Public Service that was directly responsible to Premier Jack Lang.

Anyone interested in knowing the full range of co-operatives that required the attention of Frank Jones in those years is welcome to consult the twenty-four-volume index relating to the Registers of Friendly Societies, Trade Unions and Co-operative Societies, for the period after 1911. This author was content to sample the first large volume in that series, but it provided ample evidence of building societies scattered around Sydney and all over the New South Wales countryside. Some, by the generality of their names, appear not to have been bound to any particular locality: New South Wales Investment and Building Society, Mutual Building and Investment Society, Industrial and Provident Building Society, Second Australian Benefit Investment and Building Society, and the Union Investment and Building Society. Many others had a specific locality reference: City and Suburban Building and Investment Society, Sydney Land and Benefit Building Society, Ryde Permanent Building and Investment Society, Newcastle Permanent Building and Investment Society, Clarence Permanent Building Society, Hunter Building and Investment Society, Ipswich Equitable Investment and Building Society, Mudgee Permanent Investment Building Society, Wagga Wagga Building and Investment Society, and even the Bombala Benefit Building and Investment Society. An occasional co-operative hinted at church associations, like St Joseph's Permanent Investment and Benefit Building Society, and there were examples of the popular Starr Bowkett co-operative building schemes with which Premier Jack Lang had been long associated. Sydney had its No. 1 and No. 2 branches of the Starr Bowkett Benefit Building Society, and there was a Bathurst Starr Bowkett Benefit Building Society.

Although widely scattered building co-operatives took up much of the working time of Frank Jones when he was Inspector of Co-operatives after January 1926, there were not a few other types of co-operative with which he had to make himself familiar. Among those listed in indexes at Kingswood State Archives are Sydney General Co-operative Society Limited, Sydney Co-operative Association Limited, Sydney Co-operation Hay Corn Fodder and Produce Company Limited, and the Civil Service Co-operative Society. Among the quainter names are St Peters Burial Society, and Windeyer and Meroo Slaughtering Company.[19]

When not engaged in daily toil at the Sydney office, or travelling New South Wales in pursuit of co-operative records to check, Frank Jones continued a comfortable existence with his mother at the parental home at Harris Park, and spent his leisure time on nearby golf courses. By 1928 the bachelor of thirty-four years was sufficiently financially comfortable to purchase one of the first of the stylish new American Dodge Six sedans to appear in Sydney showrooms; and we can only guess at whom else apart from his mother enjoyed motoring in style. Frank always remained extremely reticent about his personal life, especially in regard to

his earlier days. The magnificent Dodge was bought through the agency of his wartime friend in the Light Horse Field Ambulance, Bert Hudson, and it cost £598 at a time when the Public Service Lists indicate that F.H. Jones enjoyed an annual salary of £550. This was not Frank Jones' first personal automobile. His previous pride and joy in that department was a 1924 Essex Six canvas-topped touring car, bought in 1924 for the then considerable sum of £300. During the mid to late 1920s the aspiring (and maturing) public servant enjoyed a lifestyle not available to many of his contemporaries living in Sydney.[20]

Allan's Graham-Paige car

Frank's Dodge

The year 1928 was to prove a highly significant one in the life of Frank Jones. For unexplained reasons the family house at Harris Park was sold during that year, and Frank went to live with his widowed mother at a rented residence in Manly. Perhaps the ageing widow felt a need to be closer to city facilities. Later that year Frank Jones enjoyed a cruise on a French ocean liner, taking in New Caledonia and the New Hebrides. It is unclear from his own records whether this was for health reasons. However, his health was causing problems at the time. Even at the beginning of World War I, Frank Jones' lungs had been inclined to cause him problems when he was living in damp and foggy conditions. However, towards the end of 1928 an acute attack of fever and bronchitis was diagnosed as tuberculosis, a largely forgotten scourge of Australian history. Another member of the Bureau of Statistics' staff at that time would also contract the disease, and in that other case it was to prove fatal.

For Frank Jones, the diagnosis of tuberculosis was to mean several years off work, long-term convalescence in the Blue Mountains, and eventually being pensioned-off from the New South Wales Public Service (to return in a later era). Above all else, it forced him to rethink that problem of earlier days: what did he really want to do with his life? Had it not been for tuberculosis, his life experience might have proved considerably different than it was in fact to be. Who can now tell whether, as a well-paid and secure public servant, he might have married at an earlier stage of his life? Being forced from his relatively comfortable and lucrative rut in the New South Wales Public Service would cause Frank Jones to remember scholarly ambitions of yesteryear, and to return to the University of Sydney.

The family home at 6 Valley Road, Lindfield

CHAPTER 6

LIFE BEYOND THE PUBLIC SERVICE: 1930 TO 1943

On leaving the office of the Bureau of Statistics, Frank Jones was initially most conscious of his serious medical problems. He had lesions in both lungs, as well as serious throat problems. Lots of mountain air was prescribed as the only possible cure. Fortunately, those threatening lung lesions were not to link up. He moved, at first with his mother, to a small rented cottage at Wentworth Falls in the Blue Mountains. When his family moved on to Lindfield in 1929, Frank would remain in the Blue Mountains, mainly at *Coila* (the Wentworth Falls home of a Mr and Mrs Edwards) until the end of 1932.

F.H. Jones' formal retirement from the New South Wales Public service was announced in the *Government Gazette* for June, 1930. The retirement date was given as 7 August 1930, and it was gazetted as occurring in terms of section 63 of the *Public Service Act, 1902*, which presumably related to serious illness. Frank Hackett-Jones said much later that he had spent four years living in the Blue Mountains on government superannuation, and that the Government Medical Officer then declared that he would not be asked to return to an office.[1]

With the immediate threat posed to his existence by tuberculosis apparently diminished, Frank Jones was left with a government pension in itself higher than the basic wage of that time, plus a small private income from shares. Life was not all that uncomfortable, but Frank had no wish to spend the rest of his existence on the golf courses where most of his leisure time had hitherto been spent. So, he began to think of possible employment – jobs that involved less of a threat to his impaired health than did the offices of the public service.

Frank, Lizzie Jane, Aunt Bessie, and Allan at Lindfield

The family at home, Lindfield

The family at home

A Student at Law

Frank Jones' earlier associations with the student world of Sydney University, at a time when V.G. Childe and H.V. Evatt were among its shining student lights, had left him with something of an inferiority complex about his own performance and especially about his lack of facility at expressing himself in public. His early years as 'a loner' wandering around the New South Wales countryside with his Methodist Minister father had left Frank reticent and lacking in confidence in public-speaking situations. He had early learned to envy the facility with which top lawyers handled the English language. A friend of Frank's youth, Vidan Hall, had taken to the legal life, but like William McKell he had done this without enjoying the benefits of university legal studies. Hall's wife urged her husband to further his career prospects as a solicitor by undertaking university studies towards a Bachelor of Laws qualification. Vidan Hall undertook legal studies at the University of Sydney, and then proceeded to encourage Frank Jones to do the same.

Frank has left very little record of his years at the University of Sydney between 1933 and 1936, when he was qualifying to become a barrister and solicitor. His earlier (but brief) period of university studies towards an Arts degree prior to World War I may have been more exciting for him. However, it is evident from things that he later said, that those legal studies in the department headed by John (by then Sir John) Peden helped him to think through some of the tensions that had always existed between the unquestioning faith inherited from his devout Methodist parents on the one hand, and his observations of a complex wider world on the other. While his mind had been preoccupied with the minute detail of friendly society accounts, returned soldiers' settlement accounts, and later with the complex financial records of New South Wales co-operatives, the young public servant had enjoyed few opportunities to work through his personal philosophy of life. Several years of serious illness, followed by three years in an academic environment, helped him sort out some basic attitudes and beliefs.

The death of Frank's beloved mother Lizzie Jane Jones occurred on 10 June 1934 at her home in Valley Road, Lindfield, in Sydney's fashionable Kuring-gai municipality. Lizzie Jane was seventy-seven years of age when her heart finally gave in, and her elder son Frank who was by then forty-one years of age duly registered her death with the appropriate authorities and arranged for her cremation at Sydney's Northern Suburbs Crematorium. Less than four years before her death, on 2 December 1930, Lizzie Jane had written to Frank at his Blue Mountains health retreat warning him of the approach of 'the dangerous forties', and to beware the devil's snares. She enclosed a newspaper cutting of a sermon on the subject, for her son's edification. The very devout Lizzie Jane was probably aware of her son's restless mind, and that for several years he had been reading the writings of Liberal Protestant

Frank having fun with cousins, Harry and Mary Hackett

theologians like Dean Inge, Albert Schweitzer and Samuel Angus of Sydney. With his mother no longer there to worry about his dealings with the devil, after the middle of 1934 Frank could let his mind roam freely at the University of Sydney.

Like many another young Australian of that World War I generation, Frank Jones had been virtually thrown out of Sunday school into a much more seedy and savage side of human experience. The values of his old-fashioned rural Methodist parsonage home were very different to

Deck Tennis party at Lindfield

Frank enjoying pre-marital life at home and with friends

those of many of the men whom he had treated for venereal diseases as a novice soldier in 1916. A romantic view of 'the biblical world' that he had imbibed in childhood had been rudely shattered by what he saw of life in Palestine and Egypt. He encountered Christian churches on ancient holy sites that offended his Methodist sense that 'cleanliness is next to Godliness'. Measured by those values, the Moslem mosques that he saw appeared considerably closer to God, although his upbringing had taught him that they were a spiritual home to infidels who sorely needed conversion to 'the true faith'. The people of Palestine he found to be emotionally unstable and inclined to acts of sudden violence; much more akin to those ancient folk who inhabited the pages of the Hebrew Scriptures that he knew as the Old Testament, than to devotees of Christ, or eager hearers of the Sermon on the Mount.

During his second phase at Sydney University, Frank Jones' questioning of the religious assumptions of his parsonage background had been stimulated by a stormy religious argument that tore Sydney Protestantism apart. Professor Samuel Angus, M.A., Ph.D., had been Professor of New Testament and Historical Theology at St Andrew's College in the University of Sydney in those immediate prewar years when a much younger Frank Jones was over-awed by university life. Angus was then held in high respect as a scholar learned in the ways of that ancient world into which Christianity had first been brought. To the young Frank Jones, keen to further his knowledge of ancient languages and the archaeological mysteries of the Holy Land, Professor Angus had been (and would remain) an inspiring figure on the Sydney academic scene, and that relatively rare phenomenon in Australian universities – a scholar of international repute in his field.

The young public servant toiling at the Bureau of Statistics in 1914 would probably have been aware of the publication in London that year of Angus' significant work entitled *The Environment of Early Christianity*. This book was published as part of a large series of contemporary theological works, under the umbrella title of 'Studies in Theology'. We have already noted how, in the years around World War I, V.G. Childe lost his Vice-Principal's job at St Andrew's College for holding heretical social and political views, and his friend H.V. Evatt made himself unpopular with the conservative Sydney University establishment by advocating radical social and political views from a St Andrew's College base.

As Professor Samuel Angus continued to pour out publications in the early 1930s, increasingly identifying himself with liberal theological views and placing himself clearly over against those churchmen who represented a conservative Evangelical (some would say fundamentalist) position, his ecclesiastical professorial position came under attack within the Presbyterian Church. That division over religious ideas permeated the whole Protestant community, and Sydney religion has never recovered from that fierce struggle between conservative evangelicals, and liberals demanding fundamental theological adaptations to what they saw as the needs of 'the modern world'. One result of a fierce religious debate in New South Wales during the mid-1930s was that Samuel Angus was charged with heresy, and lost his professorial status within the Theological Hall of the Presbyterian Church of Australia at St Andrew's College.

As in most fierce theological contests, churchmen attached themselves to parties that then tended to polarize. The usual tendency was for members of each party to vilify those in the other as exponents of views initially represented only by extremist fringe groups on either side. By 1934 Professor Angus had added a few more letters after his name: M.A., Ph.D., D.D., D. Lit. His wide recognition as a scholar of substance only made those who considered him a serious threat to Christian faith more anxious to see him removed from a position of theological authority in the Presbyterian Church. In that year he published *Truth and Tradition*, described as 'A Plea for Practical and Vital Religion and for a Reinterpretation of Ancient Theologies'. Given the theological camps then existing within Sydney Protestantism, that subtitle amounted to a declaration of war.

In previous publications, especially *Christianity and Dogma* and *Jesus in the Lives of Men*, Angus had seriously upset those who (like Rev. Charles Jones) had adhered to traditional Protestant evangelical ways. The Pauline plan of salvation was central to that traditional position. *Truth and Tradition* grew directly out of Angus' defence of his theological position before the General Assembly of the Presbyterian Church of New South Wales in May 1934. Several quotations from revered fathers of the early church were used in the front of that book, to set the stage for a struggle between Truth and Tradition. Foremost was a quotation from Tertullian: 'Our Lord Christ called Himself Truth, not Tradition'. After quotations from Origen and Jerome, came one from St Paul: 'I can do nothing against the Truth, but for the Truth'. To the modern reader, these quotations appear to beg the question of how that varied assortment of ancients understood the meaning of Truth. To Frank Jones, the meaning of Truth appeared self-evident, and was assessed according to 19th and early 20th-century

European philosophical standpoints with which he was familiar. The essence of Angus' case was clearly stated at the beginning of his 1934 publication: 'I maintain that Christianity is not a system of dogmas and doctrines but that it is a way of life; it is the obedience of disciplined wills'. Dogma (traditional Christian doctrine) was not the essence of Christianity, but a mere by-product.[2]

Frank Jones was at that time studying the historical evolution of European legal systems at Sydney University, and that necessitated coming to grips with the thought-worlds of Greek and Roman antiquity, as well as those from which British Common Law had been derived. Sir John Peden's presentation of the essentials of ancient Hellenistic Greek and Roman world views greatly influenced Frank's reappraisal of his own position in relation to the lively theological debate at Sydney University. Frank came to understand those Greek and Roman worlds that had produced the classical creeds of Christianity, as having been completely out of touch with 'modern ideas'. As Frank Hackett-Jones, he would write to an Adelaide Methodist clergyman in the 1970s that evangelical churchmen had attacked St Andrew's College's eminent scholar 'like ravening wolves'. There can be little doubt that he understood the argument as one between scholarly Truth on the one hand, and obscurantist ancient Dogma on the other. In reality, more serious issues relating to the meaning of truth, within what was undoubtedly a complex ancient religious tradition, were at stake.

During all of his later life, Frank Jones would continue to fight Angus' cause in whatever religious context he happened to find himself. Although the aged Frank Hackett-Jones appeared to the casual observer to be a detached and extremely rational observer of the world and its ways, an emotional attachment to what he understood as religious truth continued to burn strongly into his ninth decade. He believed that New South Wales Protestantism had blindly turned its back on an opportunity, presented by men like Angus, to present Christianity to the modern western world in a form that would have been comprehensible to products of that world and applicable to their real human needs.

Although he could readily do without the ancient Dogma, Frank Jones saw clearly the human needs that the Christian Gospel was designed to meet. In a moment of unusual frankness, the aged retired public servant and barrister admitted that even that 'superhuman' archetype of 'true Christian manhood', Rev. Charles Jones, had been troubled by a secret hankering after the whisky flask. That leaning must have been like a time bomb waiting to explode the life of a respected member of the Methodist ministry of that time, with its total abhorrence of all forms of alcoholic beverage. On the other hand, such a real human weakness probably goes far to explain the power of Rev. Charles Jones as a preacher, driven zealously to 'save sinners' from eternal wrath.

The aged Frank Hackett-Jones would lament that Australian churches of the 1970s had (in his view) abandoned their proper role of 'holding out a lifeline to moral derelicts', for the less useful role of providing lifeline telephone services 'for the solace of social failures'. Whether Professor Samuel Angus' stress on 'the obedience of disciplined wills' could have been the source of salvation for many of Sydney's 'moral derelicts' of the years of the Great Depression, is questionable. Such a stance was more appropriate to middle-class citizens who, like Frank, were elevated above the savagery of that everyday struggle for existence experienced by Sydney citizens dependent upon soup kitchens for their existence. The exercise of human will assumes

Anzac Day in 1935

a situation where people believe that they have real choices. For some at the bottom of the social pile, freedom of choice has always appeared to be an illusion of the rich and powerful. Such 'moral derelicts' need a strong supportive social context if they are to stand any real chance of taking control over their own lives, and of ceasing to be a burden to others.

If those years at the University of Sydney between 1933 and 1936 proved to be crucial to the maturation of Frank Jones' understandings of Christianity, the world, and himself, they also provided the key to an alternative respectable livelihood in the legal profession. Early in 1937 Frank Harold Jones graduated as Bachelor of Laws at the University of Sydney and paid his one guinea fee to become 'a student at law' at the Supreme Court. On the motion of the Supreme Court of New South Wales, he was later that year admitted to membership of the New South Wales Bar. However, there was still the hurdle of working his way to recognition as a barrister, in years when few citizens felt sufficiently wealthy to pay a barrister's fees.

A Hopeful Barrister

Initially, Sir John Peden was sufficiently interested in his eager mature-aged law student to try to obtain him a clerk's position in a legal office. However, although the deepest symptoms of the Depression were passing, such positions remained hard to obtain in Sydney. Probably, Frank Jones' relatively advanced years made him less attractive than (more pliable?) younger persons in the eyes of potential employers. He therefore took an alternative path to gain experience, by reading with a prominent Sydney 'Master Barrister'. For eight months he did this for a small rate of pay, and at the expiration of that time continued without recompense. His role was to write legal opinions that were submitted to the Master Barrister, and thence to the client. At the same time he occupied chambers of his own, from which he conducted a small practice, largely for a clientele consisting of old university contacts and of people without sufficient funds to patronise an established barrister.

In those economically depressed years of the 1930s, a Poor Persons Legal Remedies Act had been passed in an attempt to provide a greater degree of equality of access to the law. Some applicants were entirely exempted from payment of legal fees, and the barrister only received his bare expenses, so that there was very little financial gain. The New South Wales Bar Council had also introduced an English scheme for 'dock defence'. A defendant at law could ask for legal assistance, and any unengaged barrister could undertake to act for him or her. Whatever practical experience might be gained from such activities, there was little in the way of profit to be had.[3]

Fortunately, the barrister Frank Jones still had that public service pension and a small income from shares, and lacked family responsibilities that might have made him financially vulnerable. One thing that his Methodist heritage had left with him was a strong sense of duty to the wider community to which he belonged. His barrister's role allowed Frank to feel that he was playing a socially useful role. That was fine until 1939, when two major changes occurred. The first was that Frank Jones married and began to think of family responsibilities, and the second was that World War II broke out and his tiny Sydney barristers' practice was seriously affected.

The Commonwealth Public Servant

Having done his full 'sacrificial' bit in World War I (and having damaged lungs as well as myopic vision, dubious feet, and advancing years to discourage any notions of military service) Frank's reaction to another war was different to that which he had known in 1914. Conscientious man that he was, he now had a family to provide for, and that meant abandoning the relative ease of barrister's chambers for a 'real job'. His contacts in the Legacy organisation (which helped ex-soldiers and their dependents) obtained him a post as Liaison Officer with Military Intelligence in Sydney. His role involved checking the reports of other censors of mail services, and to further check selected materials handed on to him. The censor's network did not confine its attentions solely to military correspondence. Overseas mail posted by civilians was also checked in case it should give away information that might be used for sinister alien ends. For example, when the luxury liner Queen Mary was at Sydney, all references to its presence were deleted from overseas letters. The Queen Mary was being used in massive troop transfers to Europe, and would have provided a huge target for any German submarine captain who gained information about her whereabouts. Unfortunately, this newfound role of service to his nation's security was cut short when a chest X-ray revealed the state of Frank Jones' lungs. The authorities apparently feared that if he were retained in the Commonwealth's service, he might become a drain on government funds through the reception of a military pension![4]

However, with so many young men sailing to the war zone, it was not difficult to obtain another position. Frank's next job was to be with the Commonwealth Department that supervised the supply of munitions for the armed services. He became a staff member in the Office of the Deputy Director of Material Supply at Sydney. The head office was situated in Melbourne, but the one-time New South Wales public servant was amazed at the state of bureaucracy gone mad at the Sydney branch. He was third in rank in the Sydney office, where hierarchy was heavily emphasised. The Deputy Director had his fully-carpeted office floor, upholstered swivel chair, and elaborate hat stand to suit his status. The Assistant Deputy Director also had a leather upholstered chair, with a smaller square of carpet, whereas Frank Jones had a similar chair sitting upon an even smaller square of carpet. The newcomer to this sphere of service to the Commonwealth Government obviously experienced anew some of those feelings he had known around the time of World War I, when he had found himself working among relative incompetents who enjoyed a better salary and conditions. Frank Jones considered himself better educated for his role than others around him, having once taught chemistry at school and having gained some understanding of basic materials during his earlier public service phase.

Frank's main function was to supervise the allocation of severely rationed goods. Wire wool was one such item. It was processed from wire, and wire was badly needed for the war effort. There were also scarce and highly valued chemicals under his control. Frank enjoyed exercising a little of his newfound authority when the United States Army sought a scarce chemical that was in big demand for dry-cleaning use in maintaining those spotless uniforms that so impressed Sydney girls of that era. He apparently got a kick out of refusing to assist in this aspect of maintaining United States military morale. Dymphna Cusack's and Florence James' classic tale of the wartime 'American occupation' of Sydney, *Come In Spinner*, suggests that Americans already had advantages over their Australian counterparts of that time and place.[5]

Frank enjoyed a large office setting employing some 150 staff. As in many similar situations there was great rivalry between Sydney and Melbourne offices, and Frank obviously found this boring and petty. Problems arose for the conscientious third-in-charge, when he found that a popular assistant had released the entire supply of a certain very scarce commodity. He suspected bribery or corruption of some sort, and tried to persuade seniors to replace the assistant concerned. His superiors refused to co-operate, and he soon realised that his actions had put him out of favour. Feeling heavily overworked, with much night overtime, Frank felt that his initiative and suggestions for improvement had made him a heretic at that Sydney office. Early in 1943 he decided to resign and put himself once more on the employment market, but this time in a situation where there was an acute manpower shortage.[6]

Meanwhile, there had been a fortunate change in medical officers examining candidates for the New South Wales public service. This time, Frank's scarred lungs were ignored, and he was accepted back into the service that he had left in 1930. After many years of conservative New South Wales State governments during the 1930s, the State had returned to the Labor Party then led by William McKell. McKell had long lived in Sydney's inner city Redfern area, and was very conscious of the scarcity of rental housing fitted to the incomes of lowly-paid workers. When he had first entered Parliament as a Labor member his family had been evicted from its rented Redfern home. When McKell thought that he had found a substitute home, the owners took it away when they learned his identity. McKell was thus forced to buy a house that he saw advertised for sale in a socially superior corner of Redfern.

One of McKell's first actions on becoming Premier during 1941 had been to institute a State Housing Commission to lay the foundations for a postwar attack on an increasingly acute housing problem. By 1943 there were signs that the Commonwealth might soon loosen its total ban on wartime housing construction, and the New South Wales Housing Commission needed its own legal officer to supervise the sometimes technical legal dimensions of land purchase and resumption by the State. During 1943 Frank Jones became Acting Legal Officer to the New South Wales Housing Commission, and he was to continue with that legal work until 1951 when he officially retired from the public service, just before his sixtieth birthday. Frank had found a niche in life that utilised earlier knowledge acquired as Inspector of New South Wales Co-operative Building Societies as well as legal qualifications from the University of Sydney.

CHAPTER 7

MARY McDONALD

The most significant turning point in Frank Jones' life was his marriage to Mary McDonald in 1939. Frank had first met Mary while she was a nurse at Sydney's War Memorial Hospital at Waverley in Sydney, in 1937. The deformed feet that had detracted so much from Frank's enjoyment of life as a youth were to play a significant role when it came to finding him the right wife. He met Mary McDonald at a point in his life where his feet problems necessitated the attentions of a surgeon, and what more appropriate place to have them treated than Sydney's War Memorial Hospital, with its strong Methodist connections.

Mary was descended from farming and school-teaching families living on the south-eastern coast of New South Wales, not far from Kiama where the young Frank Jones had spent a significant part of his boyhood. Mary's paternal ancestry consisted of McDonalds and Russells, both families having strong links with the land and dairying. These families were solidly Scottish in their origins, with the McDonalds claiming ancestry in the ill-fated Highland settlement at Glencoe, where the Campbell clan had once notoriously played havoc. However, these latter-day McDonalds and their Russell relatives were of the Presbyterian connection, which differentiates them from the ancient Glencoe group.

Perhaps more significant in the shaping of Mary McDonald's character were her maternal ancestors, the Bells. Grandfather Bell had been a highly respected district schoolteacher for many years, and the Bells (through her mother's influence) provided Mary McDonald with that early Methodist upbringing that would tie in neatly with Frank Jones' religious heritage. Her broad-minded mother once told Mary that, if she had not herself been a Methodist, then her children 'would not have been anything'. Mary McDonald dutifully attended the local Presbyterian Church with her family. This regular Sunday ritual involved a six-mile trip in the family sulky, with her

Happy together in Sydney, circa 1939

brothers Jack and Dick accompanying on their own ponies. Mary long retained memories of 'old ladies in black dresses with beads', and 'the wonderful harvest festivals' with their lush watermelons and huge pumpkins on display in Church. One highlight of church life was provided by periodic tea parties, and little Mary always sought to secure a table position adjacent to a goodly supply of lamingtons.

Sunday was still the Sabbath, and it was kept as a day apart, but cows always had to be milked despite any risks of incurring God's wrath. The God of the Scottish Presbyterians was usually sympathetic, and quite prepared to bend Sabbath rules where such serious economic matters as milking or separating the cream were at stake. The McDonalds were proud possessors of a piano and an organ, which made their own contributions to a Godly Sabbath, and a lady sometimes visited *Bellmont* to teach piano. Her mother's everyday deeply-felt Methodism, rather than the Sunday religion of Mary's Presbyterian paternal ancestors, left a permanent mark upon her.

Mary's beloved grandfather, Richard Henry Bell, had been born at Goulburn in New South Wales on 18 September 1853. On 15 July 1875, he married Emily Wilson, who had herself been born at Goulburn on 23 October 1855 and would live on until September of 1945. Richard Henry Bell lost his own mother, born Frances Saxby, when he was very young. He left home early to become a baker, but later took with enthusiasm to the life of a schoolteacher. His last teaching assignment with the State's Department of Public Instruction was at Marshall Mount in the South East of New South Wales, where the McDonalds and the Russells of Mary [McDonald] Hackett-Jones' Scottish patriarchal lineage farmed the land. Grandfather Bell's longstanding reputation as an effective Christian schoolteacher remains a proud part of the family heritage. Mary Jane Bell (she preferred 'Jane'), the mother of Mary Hackett-Jones, was the fourth child of Richard Henry Bell and Emily Wilson, and was born at Kangaroo Valley in New South Wales on 18 February 1882.

Mary Jane Bell married Samuel Hercules McDonald at Marshall Mount on 31 March 1903. Rev. R. J. Thomas, who was later honoured for his role in assisting those affected by the catastrophic Mount Kembla Mine disaster, conducted that marriage ceremony. Many years later, but prior to her marriage to Frank Jones, Mary McDonald (who had never previously met Mr Thomas) found herself nursing the aged minister at Waverley's War Memorial Hospital.

Mary's parents' wedding received the usual enthusiastic notice in the local press. It was described as a 'very pretty wedding', the bride and her attendant bridesmaids being resplendent in white silk, with four other sisters of the bride being dressed in white silk and muslin. The bridegroom, Samuel McDonald, had the support of his brother Fred as best man, while the congregation intoned *The voice that breathed over Eden* as a bridal entry offering. After a family-oriented wedding breakfast at the bride's former home, bride and groom shook off the clinging confetti to board the 3 p.m. train for Sydney and their weekend honeymoon. Their wedding photograph shows the bridegroom seated, with his bride proudly displaying her wedding dress. Presumably, family or friends milked the cows that weekend.

Mary Gweneth McDonald was born the sixth child of Mary Jane Bell and Samuel McDonald, at the family's farm property, *Bellmont*, Shellharbour, on 31 March 1914. It was the eleventh anniversary of her parents' marriage. Perhaps Mary's lifelong fascination with obstetrics owes something to the circumstances of her own entry into this world. The local general practitioner Dr Fox came to the farm and amused himself shooting pigeons on the day that Mary was expected to arrive. By late afternoon Dr Fox had decided that he was the victim of a false alarm, and set off homewards on a six-mile ride through the bush. The good doctor was still unsaddling his steed when Samuel McDonald caught up with him to say that the baby was on its way, and his services were indeed needed. Once having arrived, Mary was slow to begin breathing, so that Grandma Bell despaired of her existence, 'poor little thing!' – whereupon baby Mary McDonald began to breathe normally.

The young nurse McDonald

During her childhood Mary became especially attached to her surviving older brothers, John Henry (Jack) McDonald born 23 February 1904, and Samuel Richard (Dick) born 24 February 1906. Both brothers had been born at Mount Terry near the coastal hamlet of Jamberoo. Another brother, Charlie, had been born in October 1910 but did not survive. Mary also enjoyed the company of an older sister, Jean, and a younger sister named Lorna.

Little Mary McDonald was conscious of the recent death of another infant sister, and she long remembered the funeral of her stillborn younger brother, Angus, with his tiny coffin resting in a buggy sombrely driven by her father. Mary was always relieved when her beloved mother returned from solitary strolls to the little district cemetery, being fearful when separated from that comforting maternal presence for any length of time. The lingering grief associated with the frequent loss of loved little ones gave a special depth and poignancy to the Christian faith of mothers of that generation.

Mary McDonald grew up with a strong consciousness of human frailty, of the proneness of people to illness, and of the ever-present reality of death in her domestic circle. Her mother's staunch Christian evangelical faith was the supreme reality of her young life. It became such an integral part of her that she could never take too seriously Frank's agonised religious questionings, and his wrestling with what for her were abstract subtleties of Christian doctrine. Her religion (like that of her mother) did not depend upon intellectual systems, but was a practical matter of everyday experience and basic existence. At its centre was the supreme reality of what Mary Hackett-Jones later described as 'unconditional love', taught not as a proposition of abstract dogma but imbibed almost imperceptibly as a gift transmitted through her devout mother. That gift, and the understanding of human frailty that went with it, would later be passed on to hospital patients in Mary's care, and to her own (sometimes ailing or erring) children. Mary never forgot her ageing mother's response to a question put to her by Frank Jones at census time. He asked for her religious denomination, to which the old lady responded, 'write me as a Christian believer!', indicating her supreme distaste for all denominational divisions within the family of the Church. For Mary Hackett-Jones, the memory of her mother always remained that of a saint.

Mary long remembered the simple childish pleasures of her early life among the cow pastures of *Bellmont*. Her pony Daisy's tendency to nip ensured that the beast would long live on in her memory. With the first autumn rains on the warm soil there came the excitement of discovering a new patch of mushrooms, with their neat forms and fresh white and pink tones. Mary played at dolls on the verandah steps with her younger sister Lorna, emulating the careful housekeeping traits of her mother. On cold wintry nights bedtime was made more inviting when her mother wrapped one of the 'sand irons' from the top of the wood stove in an old blanket, to warm the sheets. A set of those simple and clumsy ironing instruments was a fundamental part of the housekeeping equipment of a pre-electric era. Saturday was cleaning day, in preparation for the quietness of the Sabbath. Mary had an allergy to dust, especially to that from the kapok filling commonly used in mattresses of that era, and was therefore banned from sweeping and dusting. She was however given the tedious task of cleaning venetian blinds, scrubbing off grime that so readily accumulated on the surfaces of any farmhouse bath, and washing out the bathroom.

As a child, Mary shared readily in the outdoor life of a dairy farm, with its seven-days-a-week and dawn-to-dusk demands on all members of the family unit. She had her own favoured spots around *Bellmont*, many of them given pet names during daily rounds of driving the heifers to new pasture, or bringing in farm horses for the men of the house to harness or saddle. Mary had her 'Garden of Eden', where she delighted in the sight of the shy bowerbirds dancing. These curious and acquisitive birds ornamented their nesting places with broken pieces of blue chinaware and any blue flowers conveniently to hand (or beak?). She had another favourite spot known lovingly as 'Junket', and after showers of rain Mary washed her dolls there in convenient water-retaining holes in the dark pockmarked basalt surface. Other spots around *Bellmont* had names like 'Mick's Tent' and 'Prior's House', such names probably referring to departed past-inhabitants of those localities.

A favourite childhood haunt was the old shed where the saccharine crop (a kind of sorghum) was cut up to make succulent cow feed. This made a convenient cubby house, and Mary remembered being there with her older sister Jean when the news came that grandmother Russell of the lace bonnet (wife of grandfather McDonald) had passed on. This shed also featured in one of Mary's more traumatic memories of life on the farm. Having discovered a container of treacle in a kitchen cupboard, little Mary was spreading treacle on bread for an unscheduled lunch when her mother appeared and announced that her father used the treacle to poison rabbits. In fact, the treacle was apparently used in making up harmless decoy baits. Throwing the bread and treacle to the dogs, the shocked child fled to the shed to pray, and remembered that for years afterwards 'Please God don't let me die' was regularly tacked on to her prayers. That alarming childhood experience meant that Mary long retained a deep-felt horror of poisons.

Rabbits provided such a serious threat to an Australian farmer's pasture and livelihood, that no sentiment was wasted on them. Mary well knew the experience of 'going around the traps' with her brother Dick, in the dark of evening. The steel-jawed traps would be reset in the ground, and any rabbit taken from them was quickly skinned and its pelt dried out on a wire frame for sale in town. Rabbits provided a major source of scarce pocket money to many farm children, especially in tough Depression times like those of the early 1930s.

Mary long remembered Devon the draught horse, who patiently drew the cart laden with its shining cans to the butter factory. Most of the equine inhabitants of *Bellmont* that left a permanent imprint on Mary's mind were of the lighter and more fleet-footed pony variety. She retained special memories of Tom, 'a smart horse' used on her morning and afternoon five-mile rides to and from Shellharbour School. Mary had the occasional frightening fall, but considered herself lucky that some of her childhood escapades of galloping Tom up Shipman's Hill with town kids clinging grimly and perilously behind had not led to more serious accidents.

Mary's secondary education involved a more complex travel operation. The nearest appropriate high school was at Wollongong to the north, which meant a trip of two-and-a-half miles to the railway siding at Oak Flats to board the 8 o'clock train. Sometimes, she considered herself fortunate to be given a lift by the muscular railway fettlers. They propelled their trolleys noiselessly along the rails by enthusiastically using a rugged hand-lever mechanism, in preparation for a day of toil in the sun and wind. Life away from the family farm would be made more bearable by the coming of the first telephone to *Bellmont*. It was comforting to be able to ring no. 35 on the Albion Park exchange and speak with those loved ones still 'at home'.

Mary McDonald makes her debut.

Among Mary's more vivid memories of her secondary-school period is that of being present at the opening of Sydney's magnificent new 'coat-hanger' Harbour Bridge, in March of 1932, as the Depression brought misery to many inhabitants of Sydney. Mary went as a representative of country high schools, her Aunt Gertie of Wollongong paying the expenses. Although there was plenty of health-giving food at the *Bellmont* farmstead in 1932, few farmers had cash to spare for jaunts to the city. Mary stayed with other excited youngsters at Stewart House at Curl Curl, sleeping in double bunk beds long familiar to country children enjoying a summer treat at the seaside. The children made long streamers out of toilet paper, and, being the first contingent allowed over the bridge (prior to the opening), they were denied that historic vision of Captain de Groot of the conservative New Guard Movement leaping his horse forward to slash the ribbon before the radical Premier Jack Lang could officially declare the bridge open. Mary's farming ancestors were presumably numbered among those 'decent and loyal citizens of New South Wales' for whom Captain de Groot performed his unscheduled ritual. Jack Lang had few friends in the farming community.

Aunt Gertie, who cheerfully financed this historic city jaunt for her niece from the country, was one of the daughters of grandfather and grandmother Bell, and one of Mary's mother's closest family contacts. Grandmother Bell had herself remained a very attractive woman into advanced years, when she devoted herself to needlework and 'tatting' as an old lady of her generation was expected to do. Her daughter Gertrude lived with her in Kembla Street Wollongong, where grandfather Bell had retired after years of teaching school. Gertrude worked in a solicitor's office, and was among the more fortunate of eight daughters in the Bell family.

Among the least fortunate of the Bell sisters was Aunty Hal, who had been jilted in unfortunate circumstances. Her very eligible Sydney-businessman fiancée was found to have been responsible for another woman's pregnancy not long before the proposed wedding was suddenly and quietly cancelled. Aunty Hal, perhaps understandably, never forgave the human race (and particularly its male component) for the embarrassment and heartbreak that had befallen her. She became a very sad and embittered old maid, subject to fits of depression, and has left unfortunate memories even with children of Frank Hackett-Jones who strongly believe that they suffered childhood injustices because of her twisted outlook on the world. Not for Auntie Hal that deep and abiding faith in the overriding power of unconditional love that sustained life in the sometimes struggling farmstead at *Bellmont*, where Jane [Bell] McDonald of the ginger hair and freckles provided the spiritual dynamic. Auntie Hal provided an object lesson to young Mary McDonald on the value of her mother's religious faith in the fulfilment of a dignified and joyous human existence.

Memories of Mary's father, Samuel Hercules McDonald, would be sadly mixed, largely because his was a more complex character than that of his single-minded and devoted wife. Mary Hackett-Jones pointed to a strong facial likeness between her father and the sometime Australian Prime Minister R.J.L. Hawke. She said this with an added implication that the likeness was not merely one of facial features. Her father was a generous-hearted and public-spirited man, but his family was made miserable at some points in time by his need for sexual liaison with at least one other woman apart from his devoted wife; a liaison which his wife associated with a liking for alcoholic drinks that were not welcome at the farmstead. These 'un-Methodist' leanings eventually split the family, to the extent that her father left home to live with 'the other woman' – that anonymous one, referred to somewhat irreverently by Mary Hackett-Jones as 'Old Maggie'. Far from being embittered by the situation, the saintly wife told her children that there were worse sins than adultery and instructed them that should she die first they must not abandon their father in the needs of his old age. Perhaps she understood the complexities of a tragic human situation better than her young family could.

Fortunately, his daughter Mary retained fond memories of her earlier 'daddy', from before the era of Old Maggie. Despite his lack of a formal secondary education, Samuel McDonald was a gifted public speaker, a man of independent mind and spirited action, and one long regarded as a good husband and father. In his youth he had himself endured an unhappy domestic situation created by an alcoholic father, having been the family mainstay both for his mother and his bachelor uncle Johnny Russell for many years. One reason for his devoted wife's understanding of Samuel McDonald's later lapses from grace was that she saw these as partly a result of the peculiar circumstances of a deprived youth.

Mary Hackett-Jones remembers her grandfather McDonald as an old man living frugally amid the rugged environs of Cambewarra, inland from Kiama. He was usually accompanied by a pet talking-parrot, and his heavy flannel shirts reeked strongly of eucalyptus. Mary remembers being a visitor to Cambewarra and returning from church on Sunday to be asked by her grandfather, 'What was the text?' The first McDonalds of that ilk in Australia had long before set up the Glencoe Estate in bushland near Bowral. Grandfather McDonald had for some years been in the grip of alcohol, but after his 'conversion' to the water-wagon by a Presbyterian minister he never again touched whisky. Curiously, he had first tasted whisky as a medicine prescribed by a physician, but found this 'auld' Scottish medicine too much to his taste. While in its grip he drank away his original landed inheritance on the Richmond River, hence the latter-day frugal existence at Cambewarra.

Fortunately, the bachelor brother of grandfather McDonald's wife, Johnny Russell, was very successful in the acquisition of top-quality land, and it was through that benevolent in-law that this clan of McDonalds would be restored to prosperity on their own land. Johnny Russell had taken over Marshall Mount House (later a National Trust Building) from the debt-ridden Osborne family, and when his sister's plight was made known by her friends, he brought Mary's McDonald's grandparents to live there.

Through Johnny Russell's goodwill, his fond nephew Samuel Hercules McDonald in time became the proud possessor of *Bellmont* with its rich and productive volcanic soils. Johnny Russell was widely known as a benefactor of the Presbyterian Church, and had doubtless revelled in the salvation from 'the demon drink' of his brother-in-law at Marshall Mount House. Although Johnny Russell was long remembered on the South-East Coast as a smart businessman, a first-class judge of good arable land, and a great benefactor of the Presbyterian Church, he too had another side to his character. Mary Hackett-Jones recollected that the devoted housekeeper to this ageing and crotchety bachelor, Miss Gow, did not always find her life easy. However, a big portrait of Johnny Russell had pride of place on the walls of the McDonald family home at *Bellmont*.

Mary Hackett-Jones long remembered the song her father used to sing to her when she was small, before 'the bad times' came upon her *Bellmont* home:

There's one thing I know that I love my Daddie,
There's another thing I know that he loves me,
If it wasn't for my mother marrying Daddie,
Perhaps Daddie might have married me!

Mary was widely believed to be a chip off the old block, and close to her father, which made his eventual fall from grace the more difficult for her to handle. Various figures of her childhood, from the old fencer who periodically visited *Bellmont*, to one of her Albion Park school teachers, reinforced that idea that 'father would never die while I was alive'.

As a child Mary had identified closely with the dairying environment, learning the milking ritual by practising on a cow that had recently died of milk fever. Her father had not been impressed when he caught her in the act. Mary early earned the nickname of 'the dairy maid', and became an integral part of the family milking team. She regarded herself as the radical and the heretic among her sisters, and considered her younger sister Lorna to be a little too good for her own comfort. Doubtless, Samuel McDonald would have sympathised with this 'heretical' trait in his daughter. Her saintly Methodist mother was also known to express the view that the people to be worried about in life were not those who acted out and expressed their feelings freely, but the 'jibbers' who held back and withdrew from life's hurts and conflicts. Mary was happy not to be ranked among the jibbers of this world, even if she sometimes worried about things said or done on impulse and in haste. She envied her younger sister that capacity for public speaking and public interaction that had been so much a part of her father's make-up, but which she felt had been denied to her. A nurse of that era led a disciplined life of social service, and this would eventually provide ample scope for Mary to express her strong feelings in Christian action, as her mother had taught her.

Mary on the left, with her sisters Jean and Lorna

Because of the emotional affinity between father and daughter, and the strong-minded daughter's outspoken reaction against his new-found ways, Mary's mother lived in fear that Mary might experience serious physical violence from her daddy. Although he would sometimes tip the dinner table upside down, sending its contents flying in all directions, Mary always maintained her confidence that her daddy's violent anger would not bring her actual physical harm, and it never did. She was terrified when he went off alone with his gun after a domestic argument, fearing that he would kill himself. Despite a deep affection for her father, Mary remembers secretly wishing that he would die when his manner became violent, and she felt a sense of great relief when he finally left home.

For many years Samuel McDonald had been very active on the local municipal council, in addition to farming his 112 acres of top-grade volcanic soil and tending his *Bellmont* dairy herd morning and night. With his departure from the domestic circle at *Bellmont* his elder son Jack took over running the farm, and Dick soon came back from a job in Sydney to help his mother. Samuel McDonald's long-term municipal interest in roads and bridges and rural road deviations', stood him in good stead after his departure to be with Old Maggie, and perhaps to enjoy the occasional drink in peace. Henceforth he was to be employed on the shire's roads as foreman of works.

Mary still had the saintly mother, to whom the family adhered like glue in the face of Samuel McDonald's unwelcome behaviour. Like any farm wife of her era, the mother seemed continually busy in the humdrum business of keeping a clean and tidy house for her family. She was a good cook and a gracious hostess, even when entertaining those whose presence she could willingly have done without. A farmer's wife had to be efficient in the business of preserving fruit and vegetables when in season, for family sustenance during less fruitful seasons. There was conflict between her mother's love of pretty clothes and a well decorated home, and her antipathy to the sewing machine, which was an essential tool for any efficient farm wife and mother of that era.

Each year when the time came around for the local agricultural show, a highlight of social life in any country town, the devoted mother repressed her strong feelings of animosity to that detested sewing machine for long enough to turn out new frocks for her beloved daughters. People, not machines, were her real love in life, and she freely expressed the conviction that her children were her most treasured possession'. The mother's love for her children was directly linked to her understanding of the sacrificial nature of her Christian faith. She consciously tried to reflect 'the love of Jesus her Lord' in that common everyday Australian domestic situation with all its stresses, labours, and pains.

Life with the cows at *Bellmont* went on as before, after Samuel McDonald's departure, with big brother Jack becoming something of a father substitute to the younger members of the family. Even before her father had disappeared from *Bellmont*, Mary had always been relieved to hear the sound of Jack's saddle being dragged into the house. She had then felt secure in the knowledge that Jack would be able to handle any symptoms of tantrum or violent behaviour that her father might produce. With her father's departure to be with Old Maggie, brother Jack became the mainstay of his family household.

Mary's other older brother, Dick, also symbolised strength and security in that situation; and his love for mechanical and electronic gadgetry helped to ease his mother's housekeeping burden in an age when labour-saving devices were not the common lot of farm wives. Australian farmers have always needed to be mechanically minded to survive. Such an affinity with gadgetry, especially with the slowly emerging but mysterious world of electronics, was greatly prized in the bush. However, there had been no place for milking machines on Samuel McDonald's dairy farm, there being a strong conviction among experienced dairymen that the newfangled machines would contribute to the spread of the much-feared mastitis disease; a plague that could very quickly undermine the production of a prime dairy herd.

Sister McDonald at War Memorial Hospital, Waverley

In the Steps of Florence Nightingale

In that year of deep economic Depression, 1933, Mary McDonald left her dairy-farm background behind her to become a trainee nurse at Waverley's War Memorial Hospital. The roll of trainee nurses at the back of the official history of that hospital indicates that only five of the sixteen girls who began training that year finished the tough annual introductory course. Doubtless, the depressed economic circumstances of the time partly explain the fact that the list for 1933 is by far the shortest among the annual rolls of nurses completing training at that hospital. Despite the fairness of Matron Hunter, the rules were unbending and the hours of toil long and hard. It was a case of survival of the fittest, and at times Mary had her doubts whether she was going to be among the survivors, but she was conscious of the scriptural injunction about the fate of people who 'put their hands to the plough and then look back'.

Also, Mary well knew that she was incredibly fortunate to have gained the opportunity to train as a nurse at a time of very limited opportunities. Mary was aware that she had gained entry to the War Memorial Hospital largely through the connections of one of her Wollongong High School teachers, a daughter of the Hon. H.M. Hawkins M.L.C. who was then honorary treasurer to the War Memorial Hospital. With the £2-10-0 monthly pay came an unnerving detailed report on the trainee's work record from the sister in charge. Reports could be devastating, and most trainees expected to end up 'on the mat' having to explain their embarrassing shortcomings to Matron Hunter. For slender girls, as Mary McDonald then was, the art of lifting a heavy patient was not easy to learn. At the War Memorial Hospital, there was no relief from the necessity for dusting and for handling the lung-threatening kapok mattresses from which her allergies had protected Mary while she lived at *Bellmont*.

When Mary Hackett-Jones looked back at the group photograph of those young trainee nurses at the War Memorial Hospital in 1933, she felt very fortunate to be alive. Two of the close friends who stood immediately adjacent to her in that group photograph of 1933 did not survive World War II. They were among the many nursing trainees of the 1930s later caught up in the horrors of the war against Japan in South-East Asia. Of those two close friends of the 1933 group photograph, one was among a party of captured Australian nurses heartlessly murdered by Japanese troops on the blood-soaked beaches of Banka Island, and the other died from the effects of starvation and privations endured in an Asian POW camp. Others of their friends had endured unbelievable privations of food and clothing, while forced to undergo intense physical exertion in the unaccustomed harsh winter environs of the Japanese countryside. Life at the War Memorial Hospital in 1933 had been tough, but the 1940s would provide horrors unimagined by country girls in Sydney of the Great Depression. Mary Hackett-Jones believed that she was only preserved from the likelihood of sharing a similar fate by her fortuitous marriage to Frank Jones in 1939.

Although life at the War Memorial Hospital under the demanding but generous-hearted and fair Matron Hunter seemed to involve a policy of survival of the fittest, Mary McDonald was to learn that other hospital environments could be tougher still in 'the hungry thirties'. At least there had been no lack of good food at the War Memorial Hospital. When Mary went to Melbourne's Epworth Hospital for training in obstetrical nursing during the years 1937-38, she found that matrons could be much meaner in spirit than Matron Hunter, and that nurses often did not have time for breakfast. Formidable matrons had themselves been trained during the tough times and in the blood-and-guts atmosphere of World War I trench warfare, when young Australian life and limb had often been valued cheaply. But the Epworth's matron did not have any experience in a Japanese POW camp on which to base her regime. If Mary McDonald's memories are any guide, Japanese guards were little less thoughtful of the welfare of their charges than was the Epworth's matron. Nevertheless, Mary McDonald carried on her battle for survival against kapok dust and sneezing bouts, to gain the coveted qualifications required by nurses working in obstetric wards.

Having tried Sydney and Melbourne, with the completion of her obstetrics training at the Epworth Hospital in 1938 Mary McDonald decided that she needed a change of scenery. She achieved that ambition by applying for a nursing job at Manangatang in the remote Victorian Mallee. Readers may be forgiven for not knowing the precise whereabouts of Manangatang, or of the neighbouring settlements of Chinkapook and Mittyack. Manangatang was then a very hot and very dusty drought-smitten road-junction township, situated a little closer to the salt-encrusted northern shores of Lake Tyrrell than to the Murray River oasis irrigation settlement of Robinvale. It was territory familiar to those crows of Australian bush legend 'that fly backwards to keep the sand out of their eyes'. Even the rabbits found life a challenge in that land of ever-shifting sands and sparse wheat crops, where a sustained drought could contribute to clouds of red dust threatening to block out the sun over far-distant New Zealand. At Manangatang the disciplined and frigid atmosphere of Melbourne's Epworth Hospital rapidly evaporated under a searing sun. Hospital discipline and decorum were totally out of place at a settlement like Manangatang. But Mary McDonald's interest in comparing Sydney and the bush also quickly evaporated under that sun.

By 1939 Mary McDonald was fully aware that she had other alternatives to nursing at the Epworth with obstetrics instead of breakfast, or at Manangatang with sand in the breakfast, or returning home to *Bellmont* to care for her ageing and ailing ancestors. She had gone off to Melbourne in 1937, having already become familiar with Frank Jones and his problematical feet. The complexities of her own domestic history had made Mary cautious when it came to emotional involvement with men, and the move to Melbourne's Epworth Hospital had been in part a defensive move to avoid a personal entanglement that she might later have found embarrassing. From Melbourne the youthful Mary McDonald carried on an occasional and relatively platonic correspondence with the maturing small-time barrister in Sydney, but in time both parties came to acknowledge that marriage was a good idea. Mary returned to private nursing in Sydney after her Manangatang experience and the proposal of marriage came over the telephone, which tells us something about that Sydney lawyer's liking for close-up intimate situations involving any possibilities of emotional intensity.

Escape from Obstetrics to Childbirth

Frank Harold Jones married Mary Gweneth McDonald at the chapel of the War Memorial Hospital on 27 June 1939, exactly twenty years after the bridegroom's discharge from the First AIF The engagement had been brief, the engagement ring having been bestowed on 15 May 1939. The shadows of war again hung over Europe and within three months Australia would officially be at war with Germany. The 8:30 p.m. chapel wedding took place in sombre circumstances, the hospital having been rocked by news of the suicide of its long-serving honorary treasurer, H.M. Hawkins. It was a wedding conducted amidst an atmosphere of deep mourning, and no photographs were taken. The married couple quietly departed for a honeymoon in Adelaide, which Frank Jones had in former years known as the home city of his favourite uncle – that literary-minded lawyer and amateur archaeologist, J.T. Hackett. Frank and his brother Allan had inherited a little of the Hackett property that remained in Adelaide after their uncle's death, although in the tough thirties they regarded it more as a financial liability than as an asset.

The bride mixed her honeymooning with learning to drive the Dodge Six Sedan that had been a proud possession of the bridegroom since his latter days with the New South Wales Public Service. It remained with the Hackett-Jones family for many years, and Mary found that her latter-day habit of referring to the sedate 'Dodge Senior' as 'the old Dodge' was not appreciated by its proud owner. Dodge motors of that vintage enjoyed a well-earned reputation for reliability under the toughest of Australian driving conditions, and this particular example of the breed seems to have lived up to that reputation. Henry Ford might not have appreciated that popular maxim of the writer's rural youth: 'if you can't afford a Dodge, dodge a Ford'. There can be few better ways to test a honeymoon than by providing the bride with driving lessons, and although Mary vividly remembers the experience of almost running over a cow, she obtained her driving licence at Young en route to Adelaide.

The couple travelled on by the Murray Valley Highway, which in 1939 was very different to the broad bitumen road that we see today. Cows were commonly considered by their rural owners to have a natural right of way akin to that of Hindu sacred cattle, and motorists needed to be very alert for livestock even on major highways. Naturally, Mary paid a courtesy call at Manangatang where cows were few and far between, and that maturing Dodge had its opportunity to show that it could perform in tough road conditions. Mallee roads long exercised the ingenuity of Victorian engineers and road builders, and bitumen pavement was slow to infiltrate those remote and sparsely populated desert lands of sand and broken limestone.

There was little in the way of casinos and nightclubs in Adelaide in 1939, and it is highly unlikely that the newly weds would have been interested in such phenomena anyway. They lived in comparative style at the Hotel Botanic in Adelaide, whence they ventured out for occasional trips to the Botanic Gardens or to Victor Harbour. Having tried out the Dodge Senior on the worst roads that the Victorian Mallee could offer, the young couple enjoyed a more leisurely trip home to Sydney, travelling along the dune-strewn south-eastern coastline of South Australia into the Western District of Victoria. Passing by the volcanic outcrops of that fertile Warrnambool district where Charles Jones had spent his somewhat mysterious youth, Mary and Frank decided to follow the twisting but spectacularly beautiful route known to generations of Australians as the Great Ocean Road. This road is virtually unique in Australian road-building annals, having been built originally by public subscription and mostly without government aid, as a memorial to the fallen dead of World War I. It was a road built to provide work for returned soldiers during the tough years of the 1920s and early 1930s, and primarily to accommodate the needs of sightseers and tourists rather than for prosaic commercial reasons. Regarded by many early 20th-century Victorians as an impractical 'white elephant', the much-developed Great Ocean Road today remains one of Australia's great driving experiences for tourists.

In 1939 a drive along the Great Ocean Road provided more of a challenge than it does now. Sections of the road were very narrow and bumpy, and landslides provided a common hazard to traffic on this twisting ledge cut into the sides of the cliffs over the surging South Pacific Ocean. The returning bride never forgot her experience of winding down the Otway Ranges into Apollo Bay late one night, and was glad that during her sinuous car trip above the breakers towards Lorne she was on the left side of the road. That meant that Mary was adjacent to solid cliff face rather than to a void that separated Adelaide-bound tourists from surf tumbling onto rocks or the ocean deeps far below. Continuing homeward along the Princes Highway via Melbourne the young couple enjoyed the calmer seaside delights of Eden on the remoter south-eastern coastline of New South Wales, and were soon back on those fertile volcanic lands of the Kiama district that had provided so many memories for both of them.

On arrival back at Sydney the newly weds found Allan Hackett Jones, sole full-brother of the bridegroom, immersed in study for his university medical examinations. Frank and his new bride then occupied a flat at Branxholme, while his older half-sister Bessie kept brother Allan company in the Jones family home at 6 Valley Road in Lindfield, the home that had

Allan Hackett-Jones, organist at St Albans, Lindfield

Allan Hackett-Jones with his choir

been occupied by Frank's mother until her death in 1934. Although Frank Jones held the major financial interest in that Lindfield home, his brother and sister were reluctant to move from their accustomed and commodious surroundings. They eventually took over half a house nearby, leaving the ancestral home free for the newlyweds to occupy. When Mary was ceremonially carried over the threshold to become mistress of the Lindfield home, soon after Christmas of 1939, Australia was well and truly at war again.

Rosemary's christening at Lindfield

The first of the numerous children of this marriage would be brought home from the familiar surrounds of Sydney's War Memorial Hospital to the secure environs of Lindfield. Rosemary Frances Hackett was born on 1 May 1940, her mother being prepared for the birth at the War Memorial Hospital by her friend of trainee years, Florence Salmon. An inoffensive and caring young woman, her life would soon thereafter be taken away so brutally and needlessly by Japanese troops on the sands of Banka Island. Rosemary's birth was followed on 31 May 1941 by that of Francis Charles Hackett, who as the eldest son would play a special role in the later life of the family. During subsequent war years other babies regularly followed. Phillip James Hackett was born at Roseville on 8 September 1942, and would long be a close associate of his older brother Frank. Geoffrey Alexander Hackett was born at Roseville on 17 March 1944, and would in due course of time take to his father's profession of the law. Richard Quentin Hackett was born at Roseville around war's end, on 2 September 1945. Jennifer Mary Hackett, the last of the family, was not born until 19 January 1948, being the result of a parental desire to provide a baby sister for Rosemary, the elder daughter.

Fortunately, by war's end Frank Jones was firmly entrenched in a secure new position as Legal Officer with the New South Wales Housing Commission, and earning a salary that enabled the growing family to survive at their comfortable Lindfield home in a relatively upper crust and salubrious corner of Sydney. The largest room in the house, previously accustomed only to the quiet entertainment of select guests, was turned into dormitory accommodation for a fast-expanding and boisterous family. Mary Hackett-Jones would reminisce with a twinkle that the entry of her noisy brood into those salubrious environs caused something of a stir in the neighbourhood. Frank's half-sister Bessie perforce became gradually accustomed to the notion of her erstwhile drawing room having been converted into something of a battery nursery.

The young family first became accustomed to the complexities of life on this planet in that secure environment at Lindfield, with Frank junior's childhood being largely remembered for injuries ascribed to his clumsiness: particularly a broken toe from a misadventure with an exercise bar and a broken arm. His boyhood exploits were limited by the bandaging of his hands to prevent him from scratching the infantile eczema rashes (associated with cow's milk) that constantly afflicted his skin. Although Frank would eventually make his name in the field of international telecommunications technology, the young Geoffrey was remembered by his mother as the family's electronics wizard, who knew how to pull complex pieces of equipment apart. More importantly, he could allegedly put them together again in such a way that they always worked, even if they never looked as neat and tidy as they had originally. A much older Frank Hackett-Jones Jr, when well established in the telecommunications industry, liked to ponder upon the possibility that his Bell ancestry was somehow linked to that of the famous American pioneer of telephone technology, Alexander Graham Bell. However that may be, the tendency to produce boys who enjoyed tinkering with electronic gadgetry can be noted in more than one generation of Mary Hackett-Jones' side of the family, and was very likely associated with genes inherited from her Bell ancestors in New South Wales.

When, in 1951, Frank Hackett-Jones retired from his position as Legal Officer with the New South Wales Housing Commission to a large house on the small farm at Canowindra in the central-west of New South Wales, his young family of six would be aged between eleven and three years. There would be much more space to make a noise without upsetting the neighbours, and to produce home grown food to meet growing appetites. At Canowindra the family would be increased by the addition of Rosemary Gardner, the asthmatic younger daughter of a close family friend, the Rev. Alfred Gardner. Rosemary Gardner, or 'Pop' as she was known to distinguish her from the Rosemary already in the household, badly needed Mary Hackett-Jones' nursing attention at that stage of her life. Fortunately for Mary, Frank's often tenuous health improved remarkably with the open-air life in a dry and warm climate. The humid atmosphere of Sydney had kept his much-battered lungs under constant pressure during the later 1940s, and tensions with politicians and senior bureaucrats had been further complicated by the fact that he was often struggling with bronchial infections while employed at the Sydney office. Although it meant an uncertain economic future for the growing family, Mary Hackett-Jones credited the move to Canowindra with having added many years to her husband's life span.

CHAPTER 8

SERVING THE HOUSING COMMISSION

After Frank Jones' recent unfortunate experiences as censor, and as supply officer for the Commonwealth's Munitions Department, it must have appeared a fine stroke of luck to have obtained the position of Acting Legal Officer in the recently founded New South Wales Housing Commission. Initially, the workload was relatively light, because Commonwealth wartime building restrictions along with the unavailability of materials and labour made any actual building programme impossible. However, during the immediate postwar years that situation would change dramatically as land resumption by the State government gained rapid momentum, to provide building sites for ever-larger numbers of Commission houses.

When Frank Jones entered the service of the Housing Commission in 1943 there were four Commissioners: B.H. Nolan as Chairman, T.J.D. Kelly as his Deputy, A.L. Rigby, and the architect Leslie Wilkinson. When the war ended in 1945, Edward R. C. Gallop had replaced Nolan as Chairman, T.J.D. Kelly remained as Deputy Chairman, L. Wilkinson and A.L. Rigby were still members, and Mrs Phyllis Burke had recently arrived on the scene.[1]

The Housing Commission remained a favourite hobbyhorse of William McKell, leader of the New South Wales Labor Party from 1939 and Premier from 1941. From about 1935 he had agitated loudly for the replacement of Sydney's inner city 'slum' housing, earnestly believing that 'the home life of the people is the real basis of our society'. Although he lived most of his life in the inner suburb of Redfern, McKell had spent his childhood in a rural environment, as had his first Minister for Housing, James McGirr. These men favoured small cottages on a quarter acre in outer-western suburbs, above what they perceived as Redfern's unhealthy and crowded urban-slum environment. Some sections of dilapidated Redfern housing would be demolished and replaced by Housing Commission flats during Frank Hackett-Jones' period of service, while McGirr was Premier and Clive Evatt his Minister for Housing.[2]

During the mid-1930s, various New South Wales reforming groups, initially inspired by church bodies, began agitation to improve public housing in New South Wales. Their main concern was with those so-called slums of Sydney's inner suburbs, which included many homes of members of McKell's Redfern constituency. It has been suggested that this earlier movement was more interested in knocking down the detested slums than with providing adequate public housing for lower-income groups. During the 1930s house construction in

Sydney had been less than half that for the 1920s, when 85,000 houses had been built. When war broke out in 1939 more than half of Sydney's population lived in rental accommodation, despite the alleged aim of conservative governments to boost private home ownership. Although the Depression no longer dominated people's lives, up to 10 per cent of the work-force still did not possess regular employment.[3]

The impact of war conditions following so soon upon the shock of the Depression meant that housing construction virtually ceased, and the already appalling overcrowding in many working-class suburbs became worse than before. This overcrowding was in some instances more acute in outer-western working class areas, than in the much abused inner city 'slums'. With the prospect of many young men returning home from war service to raise families, Federal and State governments began to think urgently about the housing component of post-war reconstruction. William McKell had long championed the provision of cheap rental housing for the lowly paid, had urged this in parliament while in Opposition, and immediately upon gaining office had set up the New South Wales Housing Commission as a token of future achievement in this area.[4]

McKell's ideas were not greeted with universal approval. Jack Lang, recently displaced from leadership of the Labor Party by McKell, gave the administration a hard time. Those long-estab-lished co-operative building societies with which Frank Jones had been associated in the late 1920s had been joined by a new batch of 'permanent building societies' (with government encour-agement in the form of financial guarantees) under conservative governments of the 1930s. Initially, these established co-operatives had hoped to run the proposed new housing scheme, but McKell's Labor Government with James McGirr as its Minister for Housing insisted on taking the reins. Frank Hackett-Jones believed that this attitude arose from a desire that the government should benefit from appearing to attack an acute public housing problem. He believed that at the scheme's inception McGirr only controlled sufficient bricks to build two houses, but that he 'sold' the Housing Commission to the New South Wales public 'as a great government scheme' that would overcome longstanding housing problems. Housing Commission annual reports and parliamentary speeches of the era support that view.

The co-operatives were accustomed to long years of government support, both from Labor administrations under Jack Lang and from his conservative successors of post-Depression years. Members of a building co-operative of the old type each paid weekly subscriptions, and as houses were completed they were submitted to a ballot of members. All members would have their own home within twenty three years. For a period beginning in June 1942, no building work or repair that would cost more than £25 was permitted by the Commonwealth. Co-operatives continued to function alongside the Housing Commission as restrictions permitted, and were (with New South Wales' Rural Bank) allotted a portion of the 'quota' of houses permitted to be built under Commonwealth wartime building restrictions. Whereas in the year 1940 over 8000 houses were completed in Greater Sydney, in 1943 only 582 were built.[5]

Opposition members of Parliament attacked Labor's housing scheme as ridiculous:

> to talk about the carrying out of a housing scheme at the present time that will cost millions of pounds is absurd, because every pound is required for war purposes ... Until the present war started there was much development in housing in this State, and the building societies very liberally and generously engaged in housing schemes ... until the war made it necessary to conserve funds for

defence purposes, this state had a progressive building policy ... from 1937 to May, 1941, £14,000,000 had been made available to co-operative building societies and over 16,000 homes had been pro-vided for the people of this State.

A major reason for favouring co-operatives over a Housing Commission, was that their advo-cates considered building societies cheap to operate, and thought that a government bureaucracy would be expensive. However, co-operatives did not attempt to cater for lowly paid 'slum-dwellers', as would the Housing Commission.[6]

Some, like the previous conservative Premier, were plainly cynical:

> Like 'investigation' and 'thorough inquiry', survey is a wonderful word for a government in office. We are well aware of the reason for the adoption of such a policy and it is interesting to see that the Government is following the well-trodden path of appointing boards and commissions. Nothing will come of them.

Well before Frank Hackett-Jones' retirement from the Housing Commission in 1951, such cynicism would have been proven ill-founded. However, it is true that a large and expensive new government bureaucracy had by that time been established, and that many of the under-privileged would continue to experience acute housing problems.[7]

Initially, the Commission's existence was justified in terms of an urgent need to provide housing for munitions workers in Commonwealth factories. However, its founders insisted from the beginning that it would also be responsible for:

> completing a survey of housing requirements throughout the State, for preparing a long-term pro-gramme of slum clearance and housing, and for carrying out such other housing activities for which loan funds may be made available.[8]

Given an acute lack of labour and building materials, there was little else that a Housing Commission could do in the short term except conduct surveys and prepare plans. Although the New South Wales Government periodically acquired sites for housing purposes under the *Housing Act, 1912*, there was little need for the Housing Commission to employ a full-time legal officer to supervise the legal aspect of land acquisition until 1943, when it became evident that the Commonwealth Government was about to relax regulations that had heavily restricted wartime housing projects.

The Legal Eagle of the Housing Commission

In November 1942 New South Wales's *Government Gazette* formally acknowledged that the administration of the *Housing of the Unemployed Act, 1934* (as amended in 1941) was trans-ferred from the control of the Minister for Social Services to that of the Minister for Housing, and ultimately to the Housing Commission. That Act had permitted very limited government aid to meet the needs of desperately homeless people in extremely tough Depression times. However, by 1943 the *Housing of the Unemployed Act, 1934*, proved of considerable signifi-cance to Frank Jones as Acting Legal Officer to the New South Wales Housing Commission. Numerous government land-resumption actions would henceforth take place under its provisions.[9]

Among the earliest land-resumption dealings with which Frank was immediately con-cerned was that advertised in a *Government Gazette* of December 1943:

Application in pursuance of section 8A of the Housing of the Unemployed Act, 1934-1941, having been made by the Housing Commission of New South Wales, with the concurrence of the Minister for Lands, that the land described in the schedule hereto be appropriated or resumed for the purposes of such Act, it is hereby notified and declared by his Excellency the Governor ... that so much of the said land as is Crown land is hereby appropriated and so much of the said land as is private property is hereby resumed under Division 1 of Part V of the Public Works Act, 1912, for the purposes aforesaid; and the said land is vested in the said Housing Commission of New South Wales.[10]

That particular pronouncement related to a tiny patch of land in Randwick, but in the years ahead large areas of privately-held land throughout New South Wales would be 'resumed' by the New South Wales Government for Housing Commission purposes. Once details of land resumption were advertised in the *Government Gazette*, the relevant land belonged to the Housing Commission. Such government powers have never been popular with landholders, and many landowners in and around Sydney had held land as a 'secure' long-term financial speculation. The land-resumption clauses of the *Housing of the Unemployed Act* had previously affected very few citizens adversely, but in the years after 1943 many would feel hurt or victimised.

The Housing Commission's annual report for 1943-44 indicated that a major programme of land acquisition was planned for a postwar onslaught on New South Wales' longstanding housing problem. Among the earliest activities in that direction had been the identification, with a view to acquisition, of areas suited to group-housing projects in the Sydney area. In selecting sites for future building programmes, the Commission sought land that would require the minimum expenditure of scarce manpower and materials to turn it into serviced home lots. Land owners who had been 'sitting on' substantial pockets of land close to established roads, drainage, and public utilities, became especially vulnerable to government land resumptions.[11] At that time, land resumptions were complicated by a 'war service moratorium' clause in the National Security Regulations, which meant that the Attorney General's personal permission was necessary before any land in which a serviceman had an interest was resumed by government. 'Interest' did not refer solely to ownership, and it proved difficult to work out which land was legally unrestricted by such 'interests'.

The Housing Commission was able to remove this severe hindrance to its land-acquisition programme in May 1944, by obtaining a virtual blanket approval from the Attorney General for such resumptions, which made Frank's life much easier. In 1945 it was stressed that land was resumed from servicemen only where that was essential for access to Commission sites, or for site-redesign purposes. In such cases an exchange block was offered. In the year ending June 1945, 1,870 lots had been acquired (mainly by resumption) in the Sydney metropolitan area, and a further 620 lots in rural New South Wales. In 1946 the Commission's annual report cheerfully admitted that it was much more convenient simply to 'resume' private land, than to otherwise acquire it. It noted that land acquisition, however done, 'involves many legal considerations'. Most land was simply 'resumed', because immediately upon publication of details in the *Government Gazette*, that land was legally vested in the Housing Commission to provide a secure basis for preparation of large-scale housing plans. The State's Valuer-General conducted compensation evaluations. Many landowners lacked confidence in these calculations.[12]

The young family with pram, Lindfield circa 1945 (l-r: Phillip, Frank, Rosemary, Geoffrey, Mary)

The owner was first sent a letter regarding any land resumption, and was then given an opportunity to state any valid reasons for his personal retention of the site. When, as often happened, there were disputes between owner and Commission over the appropriate price to be paid for land, the owner might appeal from the Valuer General's decision to a Land and Valuation Court, where he could present any further evidence to support his case for more money.[13]

When there was a public outcry against what was felt to be unfair government action affecting a landholder, Housing Minister James McGirr decided what action should be taken. If he did not proceed, the Minister gained full publicity for his 'generous' action. If he insisted on going ahead against a public clamour, officers of the Housing Commission had to pretend it was their decision and quietly accept public disapproval. The McGirr brothers, who each served terms as New South Wales politicians, had themselves made considerable sums of money from extensive private land dealings, so that James McGirr might have been expected to have been more considerate than he sometimes was to people whose land was forcibly acquired for government purposes.

Although arguments arising from land resumptions provided some of Frank Jones' main headaches while he served as Legal Officer to the Housing Commission, he had to deal with various other legal problems. His legal section was responsible for checking all contracts entered into by the Housing Commission, and these became very numerous in postwar years. Problems could arise over the wrong positioning of boundary fences on land that was resumed or otherwise acquired. Arguments frequently arose over the true value of land that the Government sought to resume. In areas where no land had been sold for some time past, it could be difficult to decide on what constituted a fair price. Legal problems could also arise in relation to provision of the normal services such as roads, drains, water and power to Commission housing lots.

Most resentment from landowners was likely to occur where, perhaps in order to gain convenient access to a proposed large housing estate, the Commission resumed the solitary block of land owned by a local resident. Many people in building their own home had bought two adjacent blocks of land, with the idea of building on one and protecting themselves from being 'built in' with the other, and also having the single vacant block as a long-term investment for their advanced years. Such persons could react very resentfully when Big Brother grabbed their solitary patch of vacant soil for Housing Commission purposes, and it is not surprising that they sometimes gained considerable local support for their vocal protests.

Sometimes, however, the resumption of a large parcel of land could also cause serious public controversy, and in extreme cases it might even lead to loud arguments in Parliament. Such was the case towards the end of the 1940s when the Government

Family life at Lindfield, circa 1945 (Rosemary, mother with Geoffrey and Phillip in front, and Frank)

resumed forty acres at Roseville known as the Archbold Estate. Roseville was regarded as a good suburb, and the market-garden land concerned was highly valued by its owner. When

Family life at Lindfield, circa 1945 (l-r: Phillip, Rosemary with Jennie, Geoffrey and Richard)

the Minister for Housing, James McGirr, himself inspected this attractive site he was greeted very rudely by its owner. The Minister was advised to proceed to that traditional Australian destination for uninvited and unwanted visitors – 'buggery'. The Minister of State, whose dignity was thus assaulted, thereupon decided to resume the property forthwith.[14]

The land concerned was too valuable for normal Housing Commission purposes, such as those long advocated by William McKell. However, it had been resumed. It was therefore decided to build high-class houses for public servants, built to the prospective owner's personal design, and then to sell the properties at a good price to those sufficiently wealthy to afford them. It is hardly surprising that questions were raised in Parliament about the justice of such Housing Commission resumptions; although this one in fact represented a personal decision of the Minister for Housing, soon to become the Labor Premier of New South Wales in succession to William McKell.[15] McKell somewhat reluctantly went off to Yarralumla as Governor General, after Prime Minister Ben Chifley pleaded for this self-sacrifice from his old political ally. In fact, the stipend paid to a Governor General was then far below the amount required to maintain day-to-day life at Yarralumla, so that McKell's transition from Premier to Governor General involved real financial sacrifice from a man whose background had allowed him little opportunity to acquire a large personal fortune.[16]

Very little Housing Commission accommodation of that postwar era was up to the standard of that constructed upon the Archbold Estate, specifically for public servants. Most of the few earlier wartime cottages built by the Commission had involved the use of fibro-cement cladding, in a period of extreme shortage of traditional bricks or weatherboards. Although these original wartime designs were very basic, such was the shortage of materials and funds in 1945 that all the original designs had to be reviewed with the object of abolishing 'non-essential' details. Bathrooms, lavatories, laundries, kitchens (and their equipment) were standardised, entrance halls were largely abolished to maximise living space in typical brick cottages of eight squares (slightly smaller in timber versions), and cooking/dining areas were usually combined. Tiny two-bedroom cottages were quickly constructed to meet the common demand from returned servicemen with one child for a home and backyard of their own. Various experimental houses were tried, especially versions utilising concrete and steel, but these seldom proved popular with the Commission. When novel housing suggestions were submitted to the Commission, they were invariably referred to the Commonwealth's Experimental Building Station at Ryde, for expert assessment.[17]

Small timber-framed cottages clad with fibro-cement continued to provide the main source of accommodation to working-class tenants sufficiently lucky not to be crammed into converted army or navy camp-hut accommodation around Sydney. Such Housing Commission 'temporary' camp settlements as that at Herne Bay became notorious as haunts of the socially underprivileged, and acquired a sad reputation for vandalism and criminal activity. Cottages in Sydney's western suburbs usually enjoyed the luxury of tile roofs, but in inland areas roofs might be constructed of unattractive corrugated fibro cement. Since the later 1930s James Hardie's asbestos-cement-sheet factory, situated on nineteen acres near Parramatta, had provided a popular cheap alternative to bricks. House occupants and builders alike were blissfully unaware of potential health risks from asbestos.[18]

Frank Hackett-Jones later referred to 'some tiny cottages with bag partitions' having been built, although I have not noted this feature in official reports of the Commission. Plain hessian sheeting, covered by wallpaper, had been used in earlier times as a lining material for partition walls in Australian houses. In 1948 it was decided that all cottages erected by the Housing Commission under the terms of the Commonwealth-States Housing Agreement should be offered for sale to their tenants. The price was either the capital cost of construction, or valuation at time of sale – whichever was the larger. Those privileged to buy their own cottages were debarred from selling them for at least seven years.

Sorrows of the Un-housed

Although the Housing Commission's existence was early justified by the extreme need of people at the bottom of the social pile to obtain decent rental accommodation, that aim provided more difficulties than idealistic Labor leaders like McKell had realised. Perhaps Jack Lang, with a more detailed personal knowledge of slum living and of the lifestyle and particular problems of 'slum-dwellers', had his own considered reasons for 'passing the buck' to co-operative building societies in earlier years. For many lowly-paid manual workers, Sydney rents even in the years between 1945 and 1951 represented a substantial proportion of their weekly wages.[19]

The New South Wales Housing Commission acted similarly to other State authorities in its procedures for selecting tenants to occupy a limited supply of rental housing. Officers normally visited the applicants' current homes, in order to assess their domestic virtues or lack thereof. M. A. Jones, in his scholarly study entitled *Housing and Poverty in Australia*, has vividly described two such situations where people near the bottom of the social ladder were debarred from occupation of New South Wales Housing Commission rental accommodation.

In one case a Housing Commission Officer visited a housewife with ten children, eight of them under 14 years. His assessment of that situation reflected a not uncommon Protestant response to the problems of large families, who were often of Irish Catholic descent:

> The applicant appears to have acted without restraint for many years and without regard to the security of the family she was bringing into the world.

Feminists still complain of the unfairness of a world where women are expected to take the full responsibility for such situations. If assessed on a needs basis, few women could have had better claim to a Housing Commission home than that unfortunate. However, the very reason for her serious need in itself apparently debarred her from becoming a Housing Commission tenant.

In another case, an 82-year-old woman was similarly visited by an officer of the New South Wales Housing Commission. His report on that visit killed any chance she might have had of obtaining a Commission flat:

> Applicant was of unkempt and dirty appearance, the interior of the house contains a lot of rubbish and the natural housekeeping standards are far below those required of NSWHC tenants.

Here again, we see the acute problems faced by people very low in the social pecking order, for whom even the New South Wales Government's Housing Commission could provide no adequate housing answers.[20]

In fairness to hard-working officers of the Housing Commission, they had many cases of real need, from which to select a very few tenants for limited available housing. The correspondence of Clive Evatt K.C., who was New South Wales' Minister for Housing during much of Frank Jones later years of service with the Housing Commission, contains many heart-rending letters from desperate people who hoped that the Minister might have been able to assist their claim for a Commission home. In September 1950 Evatt wrote to his successor as Housing Minister, C.A. Kelly, regarding the acute plight of a married woman then living in Bexley. While himself Minister for Housing, Evatt had promised her an 'urgent investigation' of her case, but he complained that nothing had been done. The lady and two children lived in one room, and she was expecting another baby. Both her children were sick, one afflicted by kidney trouble and the other by pneumonia. Evatt's strong pleas on the lady's behalf received the reply that the limited supply of accommodation prevented any help being given, in a situation where there were many such cases.[21]

In September of 1950 Evatt wrote another letter to Kelly, this time supporting the plea of an ex-serviceman, R.J. Mahoney of Penshurst, for emergency Commission accommodation. Mahoney, his wife, and three children between the ages of two and four years allegedly slept in one damp room, and there was another baby on the way. Given the attitude of certain Housing Commission officers to such human fecundity, it is not unlikely that the Mahoneys continued to experience acute housing problems.

Several of these pleading letters to Clive Evatt during 1950 indicate that it was not uncommon for members of families to be living separated lives due to accommodation shortages. A Mr Nixon and his wife lived at the Brighton Hotel, Brighton-le-Sands, while their two children were forced to live separately. One daughter lived with a sister-in-law at Kogarah, sleeping in the kitchen, while her older sister lived with the mother-in-law at Picton. Evatt received a reply from Kelly that Nixon's name was in the ballots for two-bedroom Housing Commission cottages. Many such cases remained in those ballots for years, although the Commission had actually introduced special 'Hard Luck Ballots' in which long-term unsuccessful applicants were given a special chance to beat others for a roof over their heads. In another case handled by Evatt at about the same time, reference was made to the serious plight of the O'Carroll family at Hurstville, where overcrowding forced the husband and four children to live in one room while the wife had to find separate accommodation as best she could.

Clive Evatt's personal files for 1950, five years after the end of the war, contain many other such examples of people appealing to him for help, in their desperate accommodation difficulties. Such requests did not always involve rental-housing needs. In March 1950 a Mr Maher connected with the ABC Symphony Orchestra was said to be living with his wife and five children in a one-bedroom Manly Flat. Maher was in the fortunate position to be able to finance the building of his own house at Manly Vale; only a supply of roofing tiles and ridge-capping standing between him and the occupancy of his own comfortable house. Evatt wrote to W.E. Dixson, the Minister for Building Materials, stressing Maher's severe accommodation plight and asking for assistance to overcome the problem. The reply duly came back that all orders for roofing tiles were handled in strict sequence.

Slums, High-Rise, and Prefabs in Postwar Sydney

Fortunately, Frank Jones did not have to concern himself directly with such sensitive human situations. However, his workload in the area of supervising legal aspects of land-resumption deals increased markedly during the later 1940s, as the scale of Housing Commission planning programmes and construction projects grew rapidly. By 1948 the Commission's annual report was stressing (for Sydney and Newcastle) 'greater emphasis upon the construction of multi-unit buildings in order to achieve the optimum economic utilisation of building sites in respect of which all essential services are readily available'. The Commission took special pride in its multi-unit project ('high rise', to most readers) at Milson's Point, North Sydney. Victoria's Housing Commission must have envied its Sydney counterparts those boasted 'magnificent harbour views', with fast transport to city work-places.[22]

Acquisition of land for such multi-unit high-rise flat projects needed to be planned well in advance of construction, because the provision of essential services to enable construction to begin commonly took two years. As Frank became aware, provision of land for such projects in an inner city area like Redfern could involve complex land-resumption procedures. Many tiny privately owned allotments were required to form a site for one large estate, complete with necessary adjacent parkland and playgrounds. The long acclaimed aim of slum clearance took on a new significance, as conveniently located sites for grand new public high-rise building programmes proved difficult to obtain without the bulldozing of previous privately owned housing.[23]

However, Sydneysiders would prove increasingly reluctant to part with their old solid-brick slum dwellings in the years ahead, and much previous slum rental accommodation would become lovingly renovated neat homes for proud owner-occupiers. Not uncommonly, this new race of owner-occupiers of inner city Victorian terrace homes would come to look down upon tenants of new Housing Commission high rise flats, which governments advertised so proudly as the modern answer to slum life. A growing proportion of migrant 'New Australians', in particular, proved very reluctant to move into modern Housing Commission accommodation, when forcibly moved out of their inner city slum dwellings.

Towards the end of Frank Jones' term as Law Officer to the Housing Commission, building programmes were expanding widely around New South Wales, and despite acute shortages of basic building materials construction continued to increase markedly. In 1949 the Housing Commission was particularly pleased with the expansion of its rural construction programme, and could boast that 109 country towns either had been or were being helped by Commission programmes. The land-acquisition programme that caused Frank Jones so many problems exploded accordingly. During 1948-49 almost 3000 building lots were acquired (largely by enforced resumption) in the Sydney area alone, the total acquired across the State being just under 5000 lots that year. At that time, the total land that had been acquired during Frank's period as Legal Officer amounted to 38,465 building lots.[24]

As Frank Jones (by then for the first time officially known as Frank Hackett-Jones) took holiday leave in preparation for retirement in 1951, a federal government subsidy scheme enabled the New South Wales Housing Commission to plan for the large-scale importation from overseas of prefabricated home units. This scheme sidestepped local labour and materials shortages, but it involved an even greater need for resumed land on which to site the new prefabs. By June 1951 land had been resumed in 164 different New South Wales country towns, and a grand total of more than 17,000 permanent homes had been built by the Housing Commission since 1945.[25]

Between February 1947 and June 1950 Clive Raleigh Evatt, K.C. was Minister for Housing in New South Wales. After Frank Hackett-Jones retired from the Housing Commission in 1951, Evatt would return to the Ministry of Housing between April 1952 and April 1954. Clive Evatt was the flamboyant younger brother of the more famous High Court Judge, Commonwealth Labor Party leader, and United Nations President, Herbert Vere Evatt. Clive, like 'Bert', was educated at Sydney's Fort Street High School, but unlike Bert had gone on to the Royal Military College at Duntroon where he had been awarded a King's Medal upon graduation in 1921. Persuaded to less warlike ways by his big brother, Clive Evatt then studied Law at Sydney University and proceeded to the Bar in 1926. He was elevated to the status of King's Council in 1935, and at the end of the 1930s when William McKell was taking over the leadership of the New South Wales Labor Party he stood for Parliament, becoming M.L.A. for Hurstville between March 1939 and February 1959. Clive was generally regarded as more left wing than brother Bert, was President of the Australian-Russian Society, and was eventually expelled from the Labor Party in 1956 in the context of H.V. Evatt's battles with the Labor Party's 'anti-communists'.[26]

Prior to being given responsibility for the New South Wales Housing portfolio in the McGirr Labor Ministry that took office in February 1947, Clive Evatt had been Minister of Education in McKell's first cabinet. Evatt was the only one of his original ministers with whose performance McKell had indicated dissatisfaction, and was dropped to the status of Assistant Minister for a couple of years before being allocated the Tourism and Immigration Portfolio.[27] Evatt was a highly regarded barrister and a strong personality, and during his period as Housing Minister under McGirr there was considerable friction between the Minister and the New South Wales Housing Commission. Frank felt himself very much the 'meat in the sandwich' in those conflicts, and found it difficult and discomforting to be asked for legal opinions on delicate issues that involved a Minister who was also an eminent King's Council.

In later years, Frank Hackett-Jones described the situation between the Minister for Housing and the Chairman and members of the Housing Commission as one of war. Apparently, that King's Medal from Duntroon had left some permanent mark upon Clive Evatt's personality. One issue that created considerable division was Evatt's insistence that each Commission housing settlement should bear a prominent plaque stating that it was the work of the Government of New South Wales. The Housing Commission preferred its housing to blend in quietly with the surrounding environment, rather than being prominently distinguished in this way. Frank Hackett-Jones found that the constant appeals for his legal opinion on highly sensitive issues required the exercise of considerable diplomacy on his part.[28]

The only evidence this writer has found of conflict between Evatt and the Housing Commission Chairman in Evatt's preserved private papers (from his period as Housing Minister during the first six months of 1950) relates to Evatt's insistence that all Commission multi-unit flat projects had to be of more than three storeys. The Chairman of the Commission, Edward Gallop, had a prior agreement with certain municipal authorities for the construction of two-storey blocks, and wished to stick to it.[29] Not all municipalities were keen on their skylines being 'marred' by towering examples of Housing Commission multi-unit construction. Evatt's concern to maximise high-rise accommodation probably directly related to his personal knowledge of the large number of extremely needy cases, and to the heart-rending stories of victims of acute housing shortage who sought his help. It was difficult to obtain enough building sites in well-serviced inner city areas, and the acute human needs of which Evatt was painfully aware could most quickly be met by building multi-storey flats.

Clive Evatt was progressive in many ways, and also supported architects like the young Canadian Harry Seidler, whose novel solutions for severe housing problems brought him into conflict with more conservative municipal authorities. By building one of Seidler's controversial house models as a Housing Commission 'demonstration house', Evatt found a way around the need for a hard-to-get council permit. Early in 1950 Evatt was writing tough letters to his Premier, James McGirr, who had been the previous Minister for Housing. Evatt obviously felt that McGirr was delaying official procedures required by 'slum clearance acquisitions' in Redfern. He demanded that the Premier forward relevant minutes from his department to the Executive Council 'without further delay'. That delay would have seriously annoyed Frank Jones' legal section of the Housing Commission, which had the responsibility for overseeing complex and tedious land transactions involved in the Redfern project.[30]

Frank Hackett-Jones survived Clive Evatt's first period as Housing Minister, but it had apparently taken some of the joy out of his role as the New South Wales Housing Commission's pioneer Legal Officer. By 1950 he looked forward to retirement from the Public Service, and in 1951 took leave at half pay to make the job last as long as possible. He would turn sixty in 1952, and thus become eligible for a normal retirement. In the last New South Wales Public Service Lists to acknowledge his public servant status, he appeared as Frank Harold Hackett-Jones, apparently wishing to have his mother's contribution to his life better acknowledged in retirement. The family had previously been known informally by the name of Hackett-Jones, and Frank changed his name by deed poll. Frank's children say that he had hopes that descendants would quietly drop the 'Jones' element. Although he made no comment on this to the author, perhaps that significant action with regard to family identity indicates something of his real attitudes towards his mysterious Jones ancestry.

Frank Hackett-Jones departed the Public Service voluntarily in 1951, at the age of 59, having had enough of the responsibilities involved in being chief of the legal section in a much-expanded New South Wales Housing Commission bureaucracy. He was a very conscientious man, with a strong sense of fair dealing and of public responsibility, and the pressures involved in being caught up in internal political struggles between the Minister and senior members of the Housing Commission had taken their toll on a sensitive personality.

By that time Clive Evatt had moved into a different sphere of government housing interests, being the State Minister responsible for Co-operative Societies between June 1950 and April 1954. In a press statement late in 1950, Evatt was described as the 'official head of the great co-operative movement of this State including co-operative building societies which can be described as the Government's sponsored private home building scheme'. He was back with an area of housing policy that had been more favoured by Jack Lang than by William McKell. Earlier Labor criticisms of the essentially middle-class nature of the co-operative scheme were forgotten, as Evatt pointed to the 45,000 families that had been assisted to acquire their own homes since 1936. In 1950 Evatt could describe the co-operatives scheme as 'a popular means whereby the working man can acquire his own home.' Given the marked increase in Australian working-class affluence and job security by the 1950s, this sort of statement from a Labor leader had more validity than it would have had when Frank Jones had inspected co-operative schemes for Labor governments of the 1920s.[31]

Whatever its shortcomings in meeting an apparently insatiable demand for more cheap public housing, the record of the New South Wales Housing Commission in those postwar years compares favourably with that of any other Australian State body:

> The NSWHC has always been able to offer a wide range of housing to those displaced in slum clearance schemes. This is because it has concentrated on the construction of a balanced mixture of inner area flats, middle suburb flats and outer area cottages so that the waiting time for these three forms of housing is approximately equal.[32]

Tables formulated on the basis of the June 1954 Commonwealth Census indicate that the peak of overseas migrant absorption into the Sydney population took place in the years between 1948 and 1951, near the end of Frank Jones' Housing Commission service. Of migrants resident in Sydney in 1954, more than 18,500 had arrived during the peak intake year of 1949. This compared to a figure of just under 3,000 who had arrived during 1946, and at the other end of that time scale, 5,120 who had arrived during 1952. This migrant avalanche into a city which had long suffered an acute housing problem arising from Depression and World War II conditions, needs to be remembered in assessing the contribution of the New South Wales Housing Commission in the period when Frank Jones was its Legal Officer.[33]

The Housing Commission staff body that Frank Hackett-Jones left in 1951 bore little resemblance to that which he had entered as Acting Legal Officer in 1943. At that earlier date, Australia had still been reeling from the shock of Japan's entry into the war in December 1941. In the hectic months of 1942 some 160,000 employees of the building and construction industries (48 per cent of its prewar strength) had joined the armed forces. Of those remaining, a large number were absorbed by defence and associated works, for example with the Allied Works Council. The construction of permanent housing in New South Wales had ground to a halt. By the end of Frank Jones' first year as Acting Legal Officer, planning was under way for the resumption of home building by the Housing Commission, but it would not be until late in 1945 that sufficient labour and materials were available to make any real start on house construction. Although houses could not be built immediately, one significant component of forward planning taking place on an ever-increasing scale after 1943 was the government resumption of suitably placed building sites. This ensured ever-increasing work for the Commission's legal section.[34]

By 1951, when Frank Hackett-Jones retired, that tiny staff which had huddled in inadequate Sydney premises in 1943 had become a large bureaucracy with various branch offices in regional centres. In June 1944, the Commission's Sydney headquarters had been moved to the Mint Building, allowing for rapid staff expansion. Government Estimates for 1942-43 had then allowed for a total Housing Commission salary and wages bill of £10,764, of which about half would come from the Commonwealth. The highest-paid staff member then was the Commission's solitary Technical Officer, on £661 per year. At the bottom of the pay scale

The Mint, 10 Macquarie Street (1962)
FHOTOGRAPHER UNKNOWN, NSW DEPT OF PUBLIC WORKS (PHOTOGRAPH COURTESY HISTORIC HOUSES TRUST OF NSW, © OFFICE OF PUBLIC WORKS & SERVICES, NSW DEPT OF COMMERCE)

were two junior clerks, whose salary rated at considerably less than £100 a year.[35] The proudest actual Housing Commission constructions at that time were five brick-veneer three-bedroom cottages at Orange. There were another 95 fibro-cement cottages at Orange, a similar number of completed fibro cottages at Bathurst, and twenty more fibro cottages (mainly two-bedroom versions) at Unanderra.

Frank Jones did not work a full year with the Commission in 1943, receiving £383 for his services. His full year's salary according to the Estimates for 1944-45 was at the rate of £532. This put him among the more highly-paid Commission employees in those early years, almost on a par with the Designing Architect who received £600 for his professional services.[36] The 'Acting' component in his official designation was quietly dropped, so that within a couple of years Frank became Legal Officer. As the legal section and his responsibilities grew, so did that salary. This was fortunate, because his family responsibilities were also expanding during that period. His legal training and experience during the 1930s had indirectly provided the once-impecunious Sydney barrister with a secure Public Service income as Legal Officer, at a time when his family badly needed it. In retirement, Frank would look back to his rural youth in agricultural and pastoral settings, and settle for life as a small farmer at Canowindra, where his young children would grow up.

CHAPTER 9

CANOWINDRA, ADELAIDE, AND
A PILGRIMAGE

By 1951 Frank Hackett-Jones had experienced enough of the complexities of life among politicians and bureaucrats of the Sydney metropolis, and sought the quieter and simpler rural context
of his Methodist childhood. On retirement from the legal section of the New South Wales
Housing Commission, he was able to buy fifty-four acres of choice arable soil on the headwaters
of the Lachlan River, at Canowindra, not far from Cowra. The homestead of *Moyne* had for-
merly been the centre of a much larger pastoral property. This quiet rural haven was situated
within reach of the districts of Orange and Goulburn, where Frank spent several of his formative years. The Hackett-Jones family would remain at the large homestead at Canowindra until
1958, when it moved on to Adelaide largely for purposes of family education.

A Sturdy Yeoman

Frank Hackett-Jones had absorbed a considerable general knowledge of the ways of the land
during his rural youth, living with a father always interested in things agricultural and pastoral. His few years working with the New South Wales Returned Soldiers' Settlers Scheme
during the 1920s ensured that he did not come to his small retirement farm with any romantic

Moyne, the family home at Canowindra

notions about the farming life. However, his feeling for nature and the soil meant that he found farming pleasant, despite problems invariably faced by anyone daring to challenge the Australian environment in pursuit of a living from the soil.

There were eighteen acres of choicest river flat, with a water table some ten feet below the surface – ideal for the production of numerous large crops of choice lucerne hay. What that also meant was that Frank constantly lived with a potential flood problem, should heavy rains hit the high-country watershed not far to the east. The remainder of the small but choice property was well suited to growing cereal crops, like barley. That river flat could produce huge quantities of lucerne during summer months. However, lucerne hay, with its beautifully sweet aroma that titillates the appetites of most grazing beasts, is not the easiest product to process successfully. This author has known the pleasure of sitting on a well-lighted tractor mowing lucerne through long hours of the night, so that it would not wilt and lose its precious sweet-smelling leaves under a hot summer sun before it could be raked and baled. That mat of summer lucerne at Canowindra could bring the good price (for that era) of £20 per ton, if safely baled at its peak. However, a whole range of things could (and sometimes did) go wrong to upset that pleasing process.

Ignoring the ever-present threat of flooding in rivers close to New South Wales' main eastern highland chain, the business of seasonal timing for the choicest lucerne product was fraught with risks. Initially, the ground had to be properly prepared and the perennial lucerne seed sown effectively. If all went well at that end of the process, the timing of all aspects of the mowing, raking, and baling process was crucial to the quality and value of the end product. A shower from heaven at the wrong moment, or a

The Belabula River floods at Canowindra.

machinery breakdown, could put the whole process in jeopardy. Once established, a lucerne patch in such ideal growing conditions could produce up to eight cuts of hay in a single year without need for irrigation if periodic floods did not intervene.

Being a retired man, Frank Hackett-Jones depended heavily on share-farmers, who used their own agricultural machinery to carry out the complex haymaking process. However, such a share-farmer was likely to have various cropping projects in hand, and probably also had contract commitments to make hay on larger district properties. The share-farmer and his plant were all-too-often busy on some other urgent project, when the Hackett-Jones crop was at its peak for haymaking. This could mean that the lucerne was 'too stalky', and had lost much of its market value by the time that it was processed. Semi-trailers would come to carry their high-stacked cargoes of hay bales northwards along New South Wales coastal roads. Good quality lucerne hay was seldom short of buyers.

Economically, life was not easy for such a large growing family, occupying a huge living space that tested the domestic capacities of Mary Hackett-Jones. During his relatively brief Housing Commission phase, Frank had paid into the government superannuation scheme at the highest rate, being well aware of the likely financial problems that would follow his impending retirement from the New South Wales Public Service. Adults of that generation did not have high expectations with relation to living conditions, and much that is now considered essential to ordinary domestic existence was then regarded as luxury that could only be enjoyed by a wealthy few. Fortunately, Frank's wife had that background of life on a dairy farm during the Great Depression, and had inherited something of her mother's capacity for 'doing without' and 'making do'. Mary also felt lucky to be among the more fortunate of her nursing generation, in that she had not been implicated in the ghastly sufferings associated with the recent war in South-East Asia.

The capacity of human beings to manage in tough situations is always influenced by what they understand to be the norms of human existence, and a generation that grew up with the Great Depression and World War II had no reason to expect very much from life. Frank Hackett-Jones' generation, early immersed in the ghastly realities of Australian participation in World War I, to be followed by depression and further savage warfare, had even less reason to expect too much. Conditions of living accepted as normal at Canowindra in the 1950s would be regarded as insufferable by many younger folk unacquainted with the hardships of world war or depression, and with expectations magnified by vacuous promises from advertising agencies and politicians.

Although the economic position for a large, growing family at Canowindra was tight, at least a farm provided ample scope to produce meat and vegetables to feed increasingly hungry mouths. More importantly from Mary's perspective, Canowindra provided a warm and dry climate in which her husband's much-damaged lungs could operate effectively. Mary believed that Frank would have died in Sydney, had he not married a professional nurse, so serious were the recurring attacks of bronchitis in that humid coastal environment. Retirement to the central-west of New South Wales was to greatly extend Frank's lifespan. When the time came to move on from Canowindra for the sake of his growing family, the need for a continuing warm and dry climate was one of the factors that directed the family towards Adelaide.

While Frank's health prospered as he rode the tractor in the sun and the wind, his growing children were also experiencing something of life in the country to offset earlier city experiences. The eldest son Frank Jr has vivid memories of carefully removing the wool from dead sheep with his brother Phillip, and selling it for a good price in town. The boys' joy that they had earned sufficient funds to purchase an engine to power a model aeroplane was rudely shattered when their father claimed the wool money towards balancing the precarious family budget. What seemed to the father to be a reasonable decision in the interests of meeting the general family need was remembered by his eldest son as the unfeeling injustice of a man who had little understanding of boys. A traditional Methodist upbringing had not given much place to what boys commonly regard as legitimate fun. There was little fun in Rev. Charles Jones' juvenile domestic experience, nor in that of Frank's. John Wesley had not given fun a high priority.

Wesley had, however, been strong on the need to 'break the wills' of diminutive potential monsters early in their existence. Breaking in children, within that earnest tradition, had something in common with training dogs or breaking in horses. Those elder sons resented what they considered the rank injustice of being caned by their father at Canowindra, at the instigation of that embittered spinster relative, Auntie Hal Bell. The traditional 'this hurts me more than it hurts you' line has seldom persuaded those at the receiving end. What seemed to a past generation to be a transparent Old Testament truth, 'spare the rod and spoil the child', has seldom appeared self-evident truth to afflicted children. The sight of boisterous young males of the species noisily enjoying themselves probably brought back to Auntie Hal horrid memories of that young Sydney businessman fiancé, whose idea of 'a bit of fun' had wrecked her prospects of a happy domestic existence decades earlier, and resulted in another girl's pregnancy. The elder daughter of Frank Hackett-Jones' family, Rosemary, has no such memories of pain, and her memories of her father at Canowindra were obviously less complicated than those of her brothers.

The big house at Canowindra also became home for a time to Mary's sister, Lorna, and her husband Alec Brown, who was still recovering from the effects of being forced to work on the Burma Railway as a POW of the Japanese. One legacy of that experience was a shattered leg that later required complicated surgical attention. Indeed, it is incredible that this man should have survived at all, given the primitive and unhygienic conditions under which his shattered body had been compelled to exist. The returned soldier helped Frank about the farm.

Another helper on the farm was a retired farmer of English origins named Bill Fulcher, who lived with his housekeeper in a small cottage not far from the big *Moyne* homestead. Bill had experience of farming in the district, and his advice was helpful and well received. Bill Fulcher had grown to depend on his housekeeper, Miss Shaw, who had nurtured his children. When that lady was ill on one occasion, and pondering an uncertain future, she had asked: 'What will the poor man do when I am gone?' Mary's response was, 'Don't worry about him. I'll look after him.' When Miss Shaw died, Bill Fulcher came to live at *Moyne*, where he occupied a convenient room next to the kitchen, and is fondly remembered by the Hackett-Jones family.

A growing family of six children caused Frank Hackett-Jones to rethink his retirement plans near the end of the 1950s, as he contemplated the imminent approach of his seventieth

The lucerne flats at Moyne

year. Elder daughter Rosemary had been Captain of Cowra High School, and was ready for university studies. Her brother Frank was not far behind, and was also made Captain of Cowra High School for the year in which the family would move on to Adelaide. Young Frank had for a brief period tried life as a boarder at an Agricultural High School but disliked the experience, and it was considered unwise to disrupt his education. With very mixed feelings, his mother agreed that he should stay in New South Wales to complete his Leaving Certificate year. When Frank Jr eventually rejoined the family in Adelaide, his mother was amused to see that he was carrying a cathode ray tube under his arm: 'it developed into the smallest TV set I have ever known'.

Having always put a big value on higher education, the father of the family was keen that his own children should not be at a disadvantage in tertiary-educational terms. To educate a large family from an inland Australian home requires more in the way of financial resources than a retired public servant of that era could be expected to possess. Rather than return to the metropolitan rat-race and health hazards of Sydney, in which most of his working years had been spent, Frank Hackett-Jones looked towards the quieter urban centre of Adelaide. Adelaide's University in the later 1950s was still relatively small, its student population of eight thousand being comparable to the student body of the University of Sydney when a much younger Frank Jones had attended lectures there. He believed that it was important for a university population to be sufficiently limited that people could still know one another and communicate across faculty divisions.

Frank wished his children to enjoy something of the carefree academic experience of Sydney University before World War I. He had many pleasant memories of the football, cricket, tennis and rowing of his student days, as well as intellectual stimulation that he had sometimes found daunting. Despite those high arches that seriously hindered his sporting achievements, the young Frank Jones had found sport a very important element in his own general education. As he said much later: 'I never played enough cricket to interfere with tennis'. His children would be able to indulge in a range of tertiary-educational training at Adelaide University, covering the spectrum of engineering, law, music, and social work.

Initially, there was the problem of selling the Canowindra property *Moyne* for an adequate price. This caused its owners considerable anxiety, as potential buyers were slow to come forward for the huge and not easily managed old house on a little patch of flood-prone but fertile soil. The fact that the east coast was in the grip of one of its periodic droughts did not help. At one point, fearing that he might not live to see the sale of the property, Frank had urged Mary to move her young family on to Adelaide in the event of his early death. From his wife's perspective, a major argument for moving to Adelaide was that the dry and warm climate could extend her husband's life span.

Mary Hackett-Jones decided to take some initiative in the real-estate business, and approached the Salvation Army, which already had one institution in the area. The Salvation Army saw more possibilities in the large rambling house for its own welfare purposes, than did most potential private buyers, and accordingly a transaction was completed to the satisfaction of both parties.

The Hackett-Jones family had the necessary finance to purchase a family dwelling at Kent Town in distant Adelaide. For its part, the Salvation Army received a substantial gift from the

Moyne, as it was in the 1990s.

sale. Old Bill Fulcher was a major beneficiary of this transaction, staying on at *Moyne* as one of the occupants of what had become the Salvation Army's old people's home.

The Adelaide Lawyer and Florence Nightingale

Mary never forgot the stresses related to moving that large family unit from rural New South Wales to the city of Adelaide in distant South Australia. Geoffrey and Phillip were put on a plane flight to Adelaide, while the rest of the family set off by road in their roomy De Soto sedan. So tired was the mother of the family that she went to sleep at the wheel of the car, and was very fortunate not to have been involved in a serious accident. Stopping overnight at the Bridgewater Hotel on 3 February 1958, the Hackett-Jones family breakfasted on watermelon before driving on to Kent Town in Adelaide, in time for the children to begin the educational year.

The large old family house at 26 Wakefield Street in Kent Town had cost the then large sum of £6,500, but the effects of inflation would make that seem a trivial amount by the time that a much older Mary and Frank Hackett-Jones moved out of that much-loved and much-renovated residence into an Adelaide home unit at the end of the 1980s.

Above: The family in Adelaide, l-r: Geoffrey, Phillip, Frank, Rosemary, Jennie and Richard

Left: The family home at 26 Wakefield Street, Kent Town, Adelaide

In 1958 this house in Wakefield Street had stood in need of considerable renovation, in order to meet the needs of a large family. Fortunately, Mary had reintroduced herself to the nursing life during her period at Canowindra. Trained nurses were scarce in that part of the bush, and Mary had been invited into the local hospital where she quickly became accustomed to theatre work in a rural setting. Once established at Adelaide, Mary set about regaining nursing employment in an urban context, her major ambition being to earn sufficient to turn her new residence into a comfortable family home. Moving on from X-ray work, Mary renewed her acquaintance with night-duty at an Adelaide hospital, where she became sister-in-charge during long nights over a period of seven years.

Having early in 1958 moved into that substantial old Adelaide family house, set in large grounds and complete with its own tennis court, Frank Hackett-Jones' mind turned to ways of using his diversified talents to boost the family income as he approached that traditional life-barrier of 'three score years and ten'. A professional training in law can be frustratingly local in its application. Although Frank had enjoyed a barrister's status in New South Wales for more than two decades, in South Australia those Sydney qualifications merely entitled him to practise as a solicitor. On first arriving at Adelaide he worked for the firm of Napier and Grubb as a clerk, to feel his way into this new working environment. When Mr Grubb left the firm, he became Mr Napier's associate. Frank was mainly involved in junior work for Queen's Counsel, often associated with divorce cases. Becoming

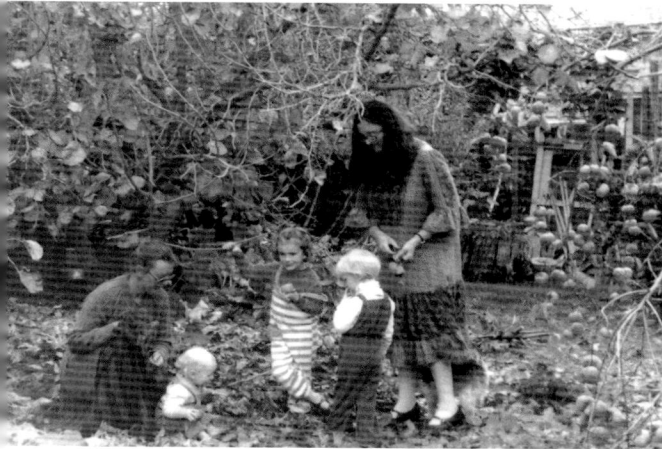

The garden at Wakefield Street, much later, in 1983 (l-r: Geoffrey's wife Penelope with daughters Mary and Emily, and Michael with his mother Rosemary)

Rosemary's 21st birthday, Adelaide 1961 (l-r: Richard, Rosemary, Frank and Jennie)

With my dearest wishes for the happiness of my sweetheart now and always.

Frank.

31 March 1964

A gift card shows that after some twenty-five years of marriage the affection is still strong.

dissatisfied with aspects of this office existence, Frank moved out, and for a time practised as a solicitor from his Adelaide home. He did not retire from the legal profession completely until 1965, when seventy-three years of age. At that time Frank and Mary celebrated by taking a trip to Europe, which he had not been privileged (or sufficiently unlucky) to see as a digger during World War I.[1]

Frank's letters to his long-time friend Rev. Alfred Gardner indicate that by February of 1964 Frank and Mary were seriously thinking about taking a world trip to celebrate retirement from legal practice. In the first references to that tour, it was referred to lightly as a 'pilgrimage to the Holy Land'.[2] The Middle East and Egypt (the biblical lands) had always held a strange fascination for Frank, and that interest had been reinforced by his own military experiences there between 1917 and 1919. The mystique arising from parental indoctrination in biblical subjects coalesced with an interest in the archaeology of the ancient Mediterranean world inherited from his favourite uncle, J.T. Hackett. Long before J.T. Hackett had died at Luxor in the land of the pharaohs, that young Australian soldier Trooper Frank Jones had used precious sick leave to visit the spectacular archaeological site. Alfred Gardner was apparently also speculating about such a tour, being informed (with tongue in cheek) by his Adelaide friend that, 'You can afford to be serious, having married off all your family ... Our children are not as sought after as yours, so it will be a major task.'

The reason for Frank Hackett-Jones' interest in 'pilgrimages to the Holy Land' was that his wife Mary had entered her name on a list of nurses planning to attend an international congress of nurses at Frankfurt in 1965. The previous congress had been held at Melbourne, and had attracted Mary's attention. Frank was encouraging: 'I should like Mary to have a complete change and the experience of seeing something of the rest of the world. It has to be done before I get too lethargic'. Frank Hackett-Jones would be seventy-three in 1965, and his planning was done in full knowledge of the rapid advance of old age. With another characteristic touch of flippancy, Frank added: 'I hope we shall be able to go, I should enjoy a holiday at the expense of my beneficiaries.'

By March of 1964 Frank had begun his travel inquiries at the Bank of New South Wales, and also with the 'very helpful' Adelaide Steam Ship Company. With characteristic thoroughness, he was also getting information from Elder Smith and Thomas Cook. He joked to Alfred Gardner that while that minister of the gospel was 'hobnobbing with the ... clergy and the masons', Frank intended to be 'restoring my soul at Dublin or earning the expenses of the trip at Monte Carlo'. The Monte Carlo bit was sheer provocation to his clergyman friend, but the reference to Dublin related to imbibing the spirit of the land of his Hackett and Thompson maternal ancestry. The 'truth' in the joke about Monte Carlo relates to Frank's ever-present concerns about financial pressures relating to his family responsibilities, and whether he could really afford the money to meet legitimate aspirations of his and Mary's declining years.[3]

Tour plans at that stage involved sailing first class on a luxury liner, probably the *Galileo* or *Canberra*. Arriving at Egypt in March, Frank proposed to spend a fortnight there and to revisit the ancient ruins at Luxor. Two weeks were allowed to 'do' Greece, and four weeks for Italy and Spain. Frank hoped to spend a few days of glorious May in London, and to proceed to Dublin for a twelve-day tour of Ireland. On the fifteenth of June, the couple would fly to Frankfurt for the duration of the international nurses' congress, and return to Britain to spend

Frank Hackett-Jones at Adelaide, circa 1965

some of July and August in Switzerland, Austria and Scandinavia. The plan involved a return to Adelaide for the approach of the antipodean Spring, in September. All in all, it was an ambitious and packed programme to be planned by and for a man well into his seventies.

A Pilgrimage to the Holy Land and Europe

As with many an ageing tourist, Frank found the actual tour experience disappointing. Rather than travelling with a vessel of the Lloyd Triestino or Pacific and Orient lines, Mary and Frank found that Greeks ('a sturdy, democratic people') were good travel companions aboard the *Ellinis*. However, Frank did not find shipboard life easy. A life that involved constant climbing of steps was 'very tiring', and the humidity associated with being on the ocean brought back the curse of bronchial attacks, from which the climate of inland New South Wales and of Adelaide had previously relieved him. Fortunately, on reaching the desert lands of North Africa the bronchitis disappeared.

Frank and Mary arrived at Port Said in Egypt late in May, considerably behind the schedule that he had originally planned. Retaining one suitcase and an airways bag for each of them, they sent bulkier luggage direct to London: 'the hall resounded with cries of "Ali!" "Mahmoud!" For me it was like old times, and I was delighted.' Travelling by bus to the Hotel Semiramis at Cairo, where Frank had last found himself as a malaria victim in 1918, the old soldier noted many roadside stalls. The Semiramis Hotel was opposite Cairo's famous Shepheard's Hotel, by then rebuilt. The tour of Egypt followed a traditional format: a visit to the 'very pitiful' Tutankhamen relics at the Cairo Museum, a boat trip on the Nile complete with a 'very foul lunch', and a tour of the pyramids with their 'rapacious camel drivers'.[4]

Thence the tour party moved on to the Holy Land proper. The plane made a big southerly sweep over uninhabited desert to avoid Israeli territory, before landing at the old city of Jerusalem, then part of Jordan. In 1948 the Jews and the Arabs had divided up the city of Jerusalem, with the modern city being in Israeli hands. Frank and Mary lived at the Ambassador Hotel, to the north of the old city and not far from the Damascus Gate. Frank noted many Arab encampments, and 'the constant threat of war'. Every piece of land was cultivated, with intensive terracing of steep hillsides and a widespread use of abundant fieldstone to build stone walls. In such terrain, the mode of preparing soil for agriculture involved the use of traditional hoes and picks.

Frank found that the historic town of Bethlehem had grown out of all recognition since 1918. It still boasted its Church of the Nativity, its Church of the Holy Sepulchre, and its many little curio shops; although some of these famous buildings still showed visible effects from the acute earthquake of 1927. The Mosque of Omar was also then undergoing repairs, the Israeli Air Force having added to the earthquake damage to that holy site of Islam. The

Garden of Gethsemane outside the old city of Jerusalem appeared to be free from these ravages of nature and war, and remained 'unspoilt'.

Frank and Mary then visited the northerly city of Nablus, which Frank had last seen whilst driving his limber wagon as a trooper with the Light Horse. They called in to the Synagogue of the Samaritans, 'whose book of authority is the Pentateuch'. That fact would hardly have endeared them to Frank, who wrestled all his life to reconcile parts of the Pentateuch with the New Testament scriptures. Frank's world view owed much more to ancient Greeks and Romans, than to the early Hebrews. He noted the priest bowing low before the 'Holy of Holies', and the cylinder of brass that contained the all-important ancient papyrus. From that settlement in the hills, the party went down into the Jordan Valley via Bethany, where Frank noted the 'new Chapel of St Lazarus'. Despite constant wrestling with the 'simple faith' of his Methodist parents, Frank remained heavily under the influence of his earliest biblical education.

Passing over the River Jordan by a modern road, near to the very ancient Dead Sea, the tour party entered the outskirts of Amman and travelled thence northwards towards Jerash. Ruins noted on this part of the trip had little to do with the Christian gospels: the Roman ruins of Antioch of Chosroes, the triumphal arch of the Emperor Hadrian dating from 135 AD, and even a shrine to Artemis. The earliest Christians had often found themselves in conflict with enthusiastic devotees of the latter very feminine deity: as St Paul had been reminded threateningly, 'Great is Diarna of the Ephesians'.

The return trip to Jericho saw Frank Hackett-Jones jolted out of that ancient biblical past, as he noted experimental government-farms producing tobacco and other crops, mostly by techniques of primitive agriculture. 'The New Jericho' was built to the south of the city that Frank had known in 1918 and enjoyed the luxury of irrigated orchards, vineyards and gardens watered from the Jordan River. Although he fitted in a visit to the Museum of Antiquities at Jerusalem to see some of the ancient Dead Sea Scrolls, Frank complained to Alfred Gardner that five days in Jordan allowed insufficient time for him to satisfy his curiosity about this mysterious and historic land that he had last seen in 1919. On 29 May 1965, the departure plane circled Jerusalem, offering a 'great view' over much cultivated land and arid desert country towards the Sea of Galilee.

Next stop was Beirut in Lebanon, where coastal-strip artefacts from Roman times mingled incongruously with memorials to men of the Australian Infantry Forces of two world wars. Like many another modern tourist to those parts, Frank noted that the famous 'Cedars of Lebanon' were not these days very obvious, but he enjoyed an opportunity to again enter into the spirit of the age of the Crusaders as he visited medieval ruins at Byblos.

Frank had come to the Holy Land with high expectations, and these appear to have been disappointed. He noted that the following ten days spent touring Greece provided the most enjoyable part of his tour. Four days were spent in the Peloponnese, with visits to ancient Delphi and Olympia. The focal points of interest on this 'most enjoyable' part of the trip for Frank Hackett-Jones were ruins of classical pagan antiquity, rather than those of the Christian era. Frank's mind owed much more to the Greeks and the Romans, than to ancient Hebrews or Hellenistic Jews. Sydney University had seen to that. The world of the Jews and the Arabs had too many associations with intellectual and spiritual struggles of his youthful past for Frank to enjoy it. That world of 'squabbling' and 'emotional' Jews and Arabs reminded him too

Frank and Mary board ship at Piraeus en route to Hydra, 1965.

vividly of the ethos of the Old Testament, with which he had always found it difficult to come to grips. Perhaps, also, it brought back lingering memories of earlier disappointments suffered in the Holy Land by an idealistic young soldier serving with the Anzac Light Horse detachments.

From Greece, Frank and Mary passed on to Italy:

> an abrupt transition from a dry land to one well supplied with fast flowing streams, fertile plains and valleys, where notwithstanding much strife over the centuries all the medieval buildings and art treasures remained unspoilt.

By that time, Frank was exasperated by the hustle and bustle of organised bus-tour life; 'pushed far too quickly over Europe in our two buses ... We lived on those buses from after early breakfast till just on dinner time'. He complained of regimentation, of packing every morning, and of 'being hurried' in general. Frank vowed that 'next time' he would travel by train and 'stay wherever I want to for as long as I like'. Rome, Florence, Assisi, Venice and Milan passed in a blur. There was just too much for an old man with such diverse interests to appreciate or assimilate in such a hurry.[5]

At Innsbruck, wife Mary departed for her nurses' conference at Frankfurt. Frank was rushed on through the Swiss mountain and lake country to Heidelberg, Bad Gotesburg, and eventually to Brussels where he rejoined Mary. Arriving in London on 27 June 1965, Frank and Mary were able to spend nine days in Eire, the land of Frank's maternal ancestors, and thirteen days on a Cook's Tour embracing the English Lakes and the Scottish Highlands. Their tour colleagues at that stage were very largely Canadians and Americans. This part of the trip was more restful for an old man, than the frantic rush past the Renaissance art and architectural treasures of Italy. Frank made no comment on those Canadians and Americans, but did note that 'the well-bred young Englishman is still a very pleasant sight'. That observation marks Frank out as an educated middle-class Australian of the Menzies era, rather than as a 'pommie-baiting' working-class Australian.

While in London, Frank indulged in a little characteristic 'sermon tasting'. He always had a love-hate relationship with sermons and preachers, but he did admire the 'attractive conversational style' of Lord Soper at Kingsway Holborn. He also went along to hear Rev. A.L. Griffith preach on 'anxiety' at City Temple, and he listened to other eminent London preachers whose sermons were compared disparagingly with those of Lord Soper. Frank was particularly receptive to Lord Soper's proposition that 'faith is an attitude, not an assent to propositions'.

This comment related closely to his own intellectual and spiritual struggles during the years of 'the Angus controversy' in Sydney. The famous speakers of Hyde Park proved a bigger disappointment even than London's preachers. Frank contended that their equivalents at Sydney's Hyde Park were more effective soapbox orators.[6]

Those sermons were probably a suitable preparation for Frank's imminent return to Adelaide, where the observation and criticism of Methodist preachers and their sermons would occupy much of his energy over the remaining years of his life. On 31 July 1965, Mary and Frank began their long return trip to Australia. They would sail back to Australia on the same Greek vessel that had originally deposited them at Port Said in Egypt. Frank, by then very keen to see the outline of his native land, was extremely relieved that their ship slipped through the Suez Canal just before it was closed by renewed Middle Eastern conflict. Frank Hackett-Jones believed that he had sailed past the Holy Land for the last time. However, he would return to Europe with Mary in 1976, as a man of some eighty-three summers. On that latter trip he indeed did things more his way than he had on the epic bus tour pilgrimage a decade before.

CHAPTER 10

ADELAIDE EVENTIDE

Frank Hackett-Jones, whose life had been seriously threatened by tuberculosis in his youth and who at various stages of his life had been dogged by other health problems, probably assumed that at seventy-three years of age he had only a few years of pleasant retirement left. In fact, he lived on with Mary and the maturing family, his very diverse memories, his garden, and his longstanding intellectual interests, for almost another quarter of a century. Like his father, Frank loved to till a little arable soil, and his vegetable garden long remained a major interest to keep him physically active.

Frank and Mary at home in Adelaide

If that ageing body was not allowed to rust, the astute and agile mind that had had so many opportunities to store up wisdom from a very diversified human experience remained active and alert. Close to the end of his life, Frank still greatly enjoyed reading, playing bridge, or a game of chess. The adversarial training of a barrister was largely applied to the edification of Adelaide Methodist ministers with whom Frank came into contact in his latter years. Well into his tenth decade, Frank Hackett-Jones still struggled to resolve those tensions between his parental evangelical Christian faith and 'the modern western intellect', which had been forced upon his attention by the Angus controversy in his Sydney University days.

Like many another of his generation, Frank saw a God-shaped gap being left in modern Australian culture. Despite his rejection of what he conceived to be a narrow-minded 'dogmatic' evangelical Protestant orthodoxy, he remained deeply convinced that Christianity was very important to the survival of western culture and society. As with Professor Samuel Angus in the 1920s and 1930s, Frank Hackett-Jones was deeply convinced that Christian pulpits of his time and place were not doing justice to 'the true evangel'. He lost no opportunity to bring this conviction to the notice of Methodist ministers with whom his latter-day life brought him into contact. Although he rejected that 19th-century Methodist orthodoxy of which his father was a noted exponent, Frank retained something of that father's missionary zeal. Also, as he looked out on the human tragedy that unveiled itself around him, one suspects that he sometimes wondered whether perhaps his father had been right after all.

Rev. Charles Jones had certainly not underestimated the potential for evil, chaos and violence to intrude frighteningly into any aspect of human existence. Methodist ministers of his generation had lived in close contact with the realities of social despair, in a society that offered virtually no State assistance to its victims or derelicts. That Methodist world view associated the devil closely with the effects of overindulgence in alcohol, and the destructive and dehumanising results of that great Australian habit were certainly very visible wherever the Church might go. Rum had been virtually the only currency of New South Wales, only a few years before Charles Jones had been born at Parramatta. Cheap spirits remained the solace of the socially isolated, or of those who despaired of a future, as is the case in numerous Aboriginal encampments across Australia in our time. And the whisky bottle remained an ever-real personal temptation to Rev. Charles Jones, himself the son of an obscure colonial innkeeper of dubious repute. When he preached about 'salvation from iniquity', there was good reason for the conviction and the passion that had so impressed his hearers. Christianity was no abstract metaphysical statement about the nature of the universe and its origins: it was a recipe for living that could bring hope and sanity into the lives of struggling souls who could see precious little reason for continuing the battle to exist.

The Missionary to the Converted

Frank Hackett-Jones' correspondence with various Adelaide Methodist ministers during his twilight years of the 1970s and 1980s reveals that he had been forced to think long and hard about the relevance of Christianity to the modern world. So thorough had been his own indoctrination at his mother's knee, that it had taken him many years to dare to question the orthodoxy that he had been taught at home and in Methodist Sunday schools as a child. In his later years he thought much about the ways in which that religious upbringing had affected his personality and his life pattern, both for good and ill. He knew the Methodist Church had shaped his mind from infancy, and he obviously believed that some of the effects of that situation were bad, as others were good.

Frank freely admitted that in his youth personal religion had been a façade to appease his parents' expectations, rather than a real force in his life. He had 'paid his half crown, and went to church on Sunday'. But if the day had been sunny, he had resented not being free to indulge in tennis or football, or to play golf. As the son of a highly respected Methodist minister, it was almost inevitable that he should have been expected to teach in Sunday schools, which he had done at Penrith and later at Parramatta. However, he had always been dogged by suppressed doubts, and had lacked any real enthusiasm when carrying out that duty.

A sense of outrage about the hell-fire preaching of Rev. Joseph Tarn during his boyhood at Kiama never left him. In his sensitive soul, that old-fashioned Methodist style had caused long-term personal stress, associated with strong feelings of sin and guilt. However, he always valued the sense of social obligation and responsibility, and the clear ethical guidelines that had come to him from the religious background of his youth. In mature years, his younger brother Allan belonged to the Anglican High Church tradition, being an organist with a love for religious liturgy and ritual very different to the starkly utilitarian Methodism of his father's pulpits. Allan also studied theology, and doubtless worked through his own spiritual and intellectual problems. However, that 'High Church solution' to the religious problem did not greatly appeal to his brother Frank.

Indeed, any church with an Episcopal tradition would have bothered Frank. The association of ecclesiastical authority and dogma in the person of a bishop was distasteful to him:

> And when I as a citizen see an announcement in the press that the Archbishop of [... ...] has issued a statement I fear that my usual reaction is to ask myself, 'What has the silly old goat been saying now?' ... A bishop finds that he is the spokesman of the Establishment, and therefore he cannot speak for himself – if he does he creates special difficulties.[1]

To many citizens of Adelaide, Frank must himself have appeared to be a bastion of the Establishment; but he probably understood the term in a more traditional English Methodist way that his father would have recognised. Methodists had long felt themselves second-class citizens in English ecclesiastical terms, standing over against members of the Anglican Establishment. In 1972 Frank was appalled by the televised image of an Archbishop in full vestments participating in a Rock Mass at St Peter's Cathedral, Adelaide. He commented that the church generally needed to become more adult, rather than more childish.

In 1963 Bishop John Robinson had been experiencing some of those 'special difficulties', because of the recent publication of his controversial book entitled *Honest to God*, which had upset many conventional worshippers both in and out of the Church of England. Frank Hackett-Jones was aware of the book and of the controversy that it caused, but did not bother to read it. He noted that Professor Walter Murdoch had remarked that the anonymous 19th-century author of the bestseller entitled *Ecce Homo*, and the 19th-century Broad Church Anglican literary man Matthew Arnold, had 'said the same things but in much better taste'. Frank did like his heretics to express themselves 'with good taste'. He therefore satisfied himself by purchasing a copy of *Ecce Homo* for sixpence, and declared this anonymous classic of a past age 'a most brilliant and enlightening volume'.[2]

In a letter of March 1966, after his pilgrimage to the Holy Land, Frank commiserated to his clerical friend that:

> I am generally in a minority of one, a radical, a heretic, rarely able to talk candidly with people, finding communion only with the folk who write books, caring nothing for the opinion of the SA brethren.

By 1972 Frank meditated on 'what an escape the Methodist Church had when I resisted my parents' desire that I should enter the ministry'. He thought that perhaps he 'might ... have done well in a monastery, in the company of say the Abbe Loisy and Derek Nimmo'; further indicating to Alfred Gardner that 'the thought did vaguely occur to me once'.[3]

Frank Hackett-Jones loved reading and chess

Frank was worried that the Church Union movement, later to produce the Uniting Church of Australia, would embrace the lowest common denominator of dogma and social conformity. He complained that, for all of its positive contributions to Western society, for 2000 years 'the Church has been wasting its strength by extolling the virtues of conformity, credulity, ignorance and superstition.' Frank's western-liberal intellect wished to declare war on myths, symbols and archaisms'. He thought that by defining 'sin and the devil' in 'realistic' terms, church pews could again be filled. He saw the churches in terms of that early 20th-century philosophical framework of 'the idea of progress'. In 1864 Bishop Colenso had begun the attack on 'credulity, ignorance and superstition'; in 1964 there was an intense public questioning of the whole traditional framework of Western Christianity; and by 2064 he hoped that his Church might have caught up with the ideas of Professor Samuel Angus (or something akin to them).

Unfortunately for Frank myths and symbols have always been a far more potent social force (whether for good or for evil) than have abstract reasoning or the principles of logic. Religion without myths and symbols has been tried before, but it has seldom gathered any following or had any real effects upon humanity. Such a religion has never been communicated to the masses of humanity. Although Frank understood myths and symbols to stand over against truth, historically myths and symbols have often acted as vehicles for the broad social transmission of important truths about the human situation in a complex universe. Using the term 'myth' in the way that Frank understood it, the greatest myth of all is that myths and symbols have been abandoned in a post-Christian era.[4]

Frank Hackett-Jones believed that the Church should be 'a revolutionary body, ... bringing good news to the great majority who have never heard or appreciated it'. He feared that his own church was something of a holy club, composed of members obsessed with their own salvation. Despite his verbal entanglements with various Methodist ministers, Frank believed that members of their 'shell-backed audience' stood most in need of conversion away from their shallow 'faith'. Although he had his own suspicions of a political system where 'any idiot' received an equal vote along with the brightest and best educated, Frank was shocked to read that the pre-eminent 19th-century Wesleyan Church leader, Jabez Bunting, had declared that 'Methodism is as much opposed to democracy as to sin'. He was reading K. S. Inglis' book on *Churches and the Working Classes in Victorian England*: 'a very illuminating book'. Frank Hackett-Jones was not a political radical, but he believed in freedom of the human intellect, and he retained a strong suspicion of 'philosopher kings'.[5]

In July of 1977 Frank was offering his minister friend, Alfred Gardner, a parcel of *Methodists*. Of that worthy magazine he declared 'I hope they will do you more good than they do me. They seem to be singularly lacking in substance'. Frank preferred to dip into that popular English Liberal Protestant publication from the 1930s, Lionel Curtis' *Civitas Dei*. The great virtue of that book, Frank claimed, was that it 'understands the Bible by applying same principles he would use with any classical literature'. Was there a hidden assumption there that the compilers of the Hebrew and Christian Scriptures belonged to an identical thought-world to that of the great classical authors of ancient Greece and Rome? Hebrew prophets, or fishermen and tax gatherers from Galilee, were not necessarily best understood in the terms of a Greek or Roman classical philosophical tradition.

Frank's reading list was maintained by regular visits to that Adelaide literary institution, Max Harris's bookshop, where he found 'remainders and discount prices more suited to my means'. Methodist rebel that he was, he still preferred books to alcoholic recreation.

> I am not in favour of alcohol at Methodist functions, or of giving in to the permissive generation by admitting that it is a necessary part of social life. It is still our most dangerous drug. On the other hand, my bottle-oh informs me that people have either beer bottles or medicine bottles.[6]

Whatever his doubts in relation to orthodox Protestant dogma, Frank had few doubts about the continuing validity of conventional Protestant morality. He was one of a great number of middle class Australians of his generation who found themselves in that discomforting position.

Frank Hackett-Jones clearly differentiated between 'holding people over the fiery pit' in the style of Rev. Joseph Tarn, and his own father's style of evangelical preaching. He believed that his father's preaching had been directed towards Christian living, rather than to the dramatic conversion of lost souls. Traditional preaching had, he long believed, a real meaning for 'the moral derelict': 'the solution to all problems was to be right with God'. Frank Hackett-Jones suspected those sections of the modern Protestant Church that appeared to him to have traded 'the Gospel for sinners' for the role of just another social welfare agency. On the other hand, many traditional evangelists reminded Frank too much of Rev. Joseph Tarn. Frank questioned whether the Almighty could really be silly enough to enjoy the sound of Billy Graham and his forty thousand voices singing *How great thou art!* He audaciously hoped that God 'does feel pleasure in observing piercing wits, active limbs, earnest inquiring minds'. The active limbs of his Methodist heritage were still prominent, along with piercing wits that Frank felt had been carelessly omitted from that Methodist heritage.[7]

For all his self-claimed 'radicalism' in matters religious, Frank showed few signs of social or political radicalism. He rejected what he perceived as a current view that Jesus Christ was 'a sort of celestial Lech Walesa or Bill Hayden'.

> If wealth were distributed evenly among the population, the effects would probably be far from beneficial. Jesus advised people to be content with their wages, but organised labour makes a virtue of discontent.[8]

Frank still believed in a simple 'Religion of Jesus' that had been mystified by St Paul and his successors. This standpoint has usually ignored the fact that the Pauline writings provide our earliest extant source materials on the nature of primitive Christianity. He admired 'the down-to-earthness of Jesus and those who followed him in Palestine, their emphasis on the social significance of religious belief'. That 'social significance' was obviously perceived in a different manner from that in which Lech Walesa understood it. Above all else, Frank valued what he understood to have been the apostles' vision of the Kingdom of God as the manifestation of His laws in this world, which vision 'made sense to ordinary people where Paul's occultism went right over their heads'. He had been reading Schonfield's book, *Those Incredible Christians*. There is a tendency for all of us 'to make God in our own image', and Frank tended to manufacture his God on the model of 'the great lawyer'. There is, of course, plenty of precedent in Judaeo-Christian thought for that tendency.[9]

The aged Frank Hackett-Jones was very glad that he had declined his father's request that he should become a minister of the Gospel: 'I had forced myself into a mould of conformity and unquestioning belief, but I still had a romantic sympathy for those unbelievers who braved hell-fire in their search for truth, though I did not read their books'. Obviously, it would have been impossible for him to preach from the pulpit with conviction, as his father had long done.[10]

World War I had killed any real chance that Frank might stay aligned with the faith of his father. Experiences in Palestine had obviously made a shattering impact upon the residue of his Sunday school 'Christian Education':

> The Holy Land ceased to be inhabited by people wearing haloes, and Christian churches, with their tawdriness and incense, compared unfavourably with Mohammedan mosques. I retain an impression of the uncompromising and passionate nature of the inhabitants of the region, very like the Israelites of old.[11]

During his second university phase in the 1930s, Frank had read widely in religious literature, especially the writings of such Liberal Christians as Dean Inge, and that Protestant rebel against traditional evangelical orthodoxy, Albert Schweitzer. Frank's highly logical legal training separated him further from the simple world of those who inhabited the pages of the Bible, with its vivid and even childlike picture language, and he became less patient with people whose lives were ruled by emotion rather than by trained reason. From being holy and unquestionable, religious doctrines (dogmas) had come to be seen as dispensable with changing times and 'the march of mind'.

Because he never made any formal study of theology, Franks' religious thought remained at a level where many modern theological students begin to develop their ideas about Christianity. With respect to our heritage from the Christian Greeks and the Christian Romans, Frank believed that 'orthodoxy urges us to believe both', but that our minds were incapable of understanding either. He saw modern man occupying a totally different thought-world: 'We are less speculative, more interested in psychology and practical considerations'. Perhaps it is a pity that Frank never studied the Hebrew language and literature. He might have discovered that they were something like that too.[12]

Modern biblical scholarship has moved on far from the world of 'the Angus controversy', particularly in trying to understand the Hebrew and Semitic thought-worlds of the biblical records. Whereas biblical scholars today see the Bible as a product of a long historical development out of an intricate network of ancient Middle Eastern religious beliefs, through the earliest phases of Hellenistic and Roman intellectual influences, Frank was largely concerned about how to reconcile the 'immorality' of certain Old Testament books and what he conceived to be the mind-boggling 'mysticism' of the more complex of 'the Pauline Epistles', with the transparent ethical idealism of the Sermon on the Mount. He was concerned that, in the minds of most of the Methodist ministers and lay people whom he encountered, the Bible remained a monolithic slab of Holy Writ such as his father had preached from. Presumably, his brother Allan would have been able to move more comfortably out of that narrow Protestant evangelical family background, through his formal studies in theology at the University of Sydney.

Frank rightly concluded 'that there is a considerable pagan element in traditional Christianity'. Christianity subsumed the pagan world, not by abolishing alien cultures, but by 'capturing' them and subverting their most cherished symbols and rituals to Christian ends. Frank in his old age believed that 'the Bible is a very human document, containing a great deal of spiritual value, but to be read with discrimination'. That seems to be self-evident, but perhaps Adelaide Methodism of the 1960s and 1970s was more intellectually blindfolded than I realise? It is fascinating to see that long defunct 'Angus Case' being lived out so passionately, relatively recently, in the letters of a very old man who had experienced more of life than most of us might expect.[13]

Frank's rigorous training in law and logic made it hard for him to appreciate the background to the Christian sermon, having deep roots in Hebrew thinking with its poetry and picture language. He delighted in belabouring the Adelaide clergy with a pet notion that the sermon 'as a form of religious edification … is just not good enough'. I suspect that he had a lot of silent supporters. However, it appears highly doubtful that a large-scale multiplication of disciples of that learned and earnest western mind, Professor Samuel Angus of Sydney's St Andrew's College, could have caused our church pews to overflow with earnest hearers of 'the Word of the Lord'.

The Christian pulpit was never intended to be a lecture rostrum, a debater's platform, nor even a place for teaching people 'proper moral laws'. The appeal of the Bible to humanity is akin to the appeal of great literature or drama, more like that of William Shakespeare. Its appeal is not primarily to the learned of this world (although they too may learn from it) but to the whole crazy range of humankind, many of whom have been helped by its pages to bring sanity into otherwise meaningless or tragic existences. Western art and drama and music would be left poverty-stricken, if that which has been inspired by Christian faith and literature were excised. A generation that does not understand this has lost contact with something that has long been at the formative heart of Western culture, and without which that culture can hardly long survive. In an age dominated by television, exactly what public role is left for the Church pulpit is certainly not so clear as it once was. Frank Hackett-Jones was certainly right to be perplexed about what Christianity (or its lack) might mean in his and our times.

The Limits of Heresy

Although Frank's letters to his minister friends did not have much to say about his political leanings in the age of the Vietnam War, there is enough to indicate that a love of law and order left little room for sympathy with political radicals. In 1971 Frank indicated to Alfred Gardner that:

> I rejoice to know that your Albert Langer has been sentenced to a sizeable term of imprisonment for inciting radicals to commit acts of violence.

Radicalism in the world of ideas was one thing, but radicalism that might be transformed into actual physical violence was another matter altogether.[14]

In 1974, with Gough Whitlam's Labor government enjoying the novel experience of being in power at Canberra, Frank Hackett-Jones was obviously not enthusiastic about Australia's political future:

> I should like the Liberals to win the election, but I can't be worried about it. I have little faith in the judgement of an under-educated democracy, and I am really more interested in Joshua.

Joshua, of course, was the ancient Hebrew warrior leader who caused the sun to stand still, while his armies committed mayhem upon those erstwhile inhabitants of the land of Canaan who could find no darkness into which to flee. Not that Frank was a great admirer of Joshua or his military tactics. He was concerned and angry that an Adelaide Methodist minister still found Joshua's bloodthirsty exploits good sermon material.[15]

Two months previously Frank had confided in his friend that:

> Britain's political and economic troubles were foreseen a century ago by those who opposed universal suffrage, and saw it as leading to mob rule. Economic breakdown if it goes far enough could need a drastic remedy, eg. a coalition government with a stringent prices-and-income policy, or a dictatorship of some kind.[16]

Eminent ancient Greek philosophers had shared those fears that have a sound basis in the political history of human societies. However,

Frank keeps up with the news, Adelaide

Australians in the 1970s did not often express them. Perhaps Frank's advancing years contributed to his deep pessimism about the political future of Australia.

Politicians, whatever their party affiliation might be, who offended Frank's sense of good taste in the use of the English language, were sure to draw his fire:

> Re Peacock, M.H.R. and his grammar, this is a matter which hits me where it hurts. There seems to be a conspiracy to use the nominative pronoun after a preposition. Even after a verb at times ... It is a fault which could not be committed by anyone who had read such examples of English as the Bible or the Book of Common Prayer.

Whatever Frank's distaste for ancient dogma and superstition enshrined in Christian scripture or classic liturgies, such documents in 'the King's English' remained vital reading for all aspiring orators or politicians.[17]

As for poetry, it had ceased to be produced at about the time of World War I:

> I can work up no enthusiasm for modern poetry. It lacks subject matter. Their predecessors, up to the wartime poets of 1914, had something to write about.

Frank considered that Browning 'should be compulsory reading for people of my age'. By comparison, he thought that 'most modern poets have no subject matter'. Not for him the music of words and phrases, without something for his logical processes to chew upon. When Frank really wished to assault 'modernity', he turned upon that universal symbol of modern life and death, the automobile: 'I wish its evil potentialities had been recognised seventy years ago, and its manufacture and use greatly restricted'. That was fine for Frank. He had enjoyed the regular use of motor vehicles long before most Australians had known the opportunity.[18]

Frank 'gives Rosemary away', with sister Jennie as bridesmaid (1966)

An Ageing Patriarch Guides his Flock

Fortunately, Frank Hackett-Jones had his large and maturing family to distract his mind from sermons on the bloody exploits of Joshua, from the carnage of automobiles, and from the murder of the Queen's English by politicians and media personalities. In September of 1966, one letter noted that his elder daughter Rosemary and new son-in-law Melvyn Cann would be boarding an aeroplane for London, en route to Oxford. Melvyn, a bright product of Professor Jack Smart's Adelaide University Philosophy Department, was off to Oxford on a Commonwealth United Kingdom Scholarship to pursue postgraduate studies under the guidance of the eminent philosopher, A.J. Ayer. Melvyn shared with Rosemary a deep interest in music, and his love for the violin sometimes distracted him from philosophical pursuits at Oxford and in Melbourne.

Frank, as her father, was more concerned about how Rosemary would cope with her new situation. He imagined that her major problem would be in becoming a housewife after her 'busy life'. This author, having been privileged to be entertained by Rosemary and Melvyn at their Boar's Hill home near Oxford, and having seen Rosemary's kitchen afterwards, can attest that her father's concern was not totally devoid of substance. In July of 1969, Frank was following with interest the travels of Rosemary and Melvyn and baby Rachel, as they wended their way through Vienna and Genoa, prior to embarking on a ship for return to Australia. Melvyn returned to a lectureship in Philosophy at the then very young La Trobe University, situated to the north of Melbourne. Melbourne was not Adelaide, but with shrinking academic employment opportunities at that time, Frank's daughter could have been much further away.[19]

The eldest son, Frank Jr. also kept his father's mind active by his travels around the globe. Since the farming days at Canowindra, Frank Jr had been his father's ready helper around the place. In July 1971 the proud father noted that his boy was on a trip via the United States to Mexico, Brazil, and Argentina, and was procuring useful contracts for the company in whose interests he travelled. Frank Jr had initially accompanied his talented new wife Geraldine to Europe, in order to further her singing opportunities. His engineering background drew him into the international telecommunications industry, and while his wife spent long periods of time at singing rehearsals Frank was seeking contracts in South America. The ageing Frank Hackett-Jones pondered on how compatible two such very different and time-consuming professional lives could be. By July of 1971 he was telling his minister friend of Geraldine's impending participation in *Master Class* in London: 'the programme which is televised here by the ABC on Sunday afternoons'. His letters followed her around the Hague, Munich, Dusseldorf and Frankfort, and back to London where she had been invited to sing with The Fine Arts Orchestra.[20]

The four other children of Frank and Mary flitted through the correspondence periodically. In July of 1967 Richard had spent more than fifteen months in the army, and 'was still at Canungra'. He was of the generation that found its names inserted into a ballot box, with the prospect of compulsory national military service in the Vietnam War as the doubtful prize of random selection.

Jennifer, the baby of the family, had just passed her driving test which would make her 'a handy chauffeuse' when circumstances forced Frank to utilise that dangerous mechanical abomination, the automobile. By July 1971 Frank noted that Jennifer had bought a book entitled *Teach Yourself Latvian*. Before long Frank and Mary would be hosting her wedding to Andris Bandes, a young Adelaide man of Latvian descent: 'Jennifer's wedding is the most important event in the future'. As he reached advanced years, Frank Hackett Jones was happy to see his adult children married.[21]

Geoffrey, the budding Adelaide lawyer who had earlier shown an aptitude for electronic tinkering, had allegedly procured a volume of English love poems, 'and has, we hope, taken to courting'. Geoffrey's subsequent marriage to Penelope Temby at Kent Town Methodist Church

Frank and Mary in their front garden with son Geoffrey on his wedding day in 1973

Frank with Geoffrey, Mary and Emily a few months after his appointment as Queen's Counsel in 1986.

in December of 1973 indicates that his father was not entirely devoid of perceptiveness in these matters. At that time his father was also indicating an interest in Richard's recent venture into the business of selling insurance in Adelaide, which vocation he seemed to consider almost as hazardous as getting married.[22]

Frank with granddaughter Francesca at Adelaide, 1970

Later in 1971 a letter to Alfred Gardner indicated that Phillip, the second eldest son, had resigned his hospital job with the intention of trying life on the high seas as a commercial fisherman. That venture into a business partnership dependent on the seasonal vagaries of trawling the fruits of the great deep was short-lived. By September 1972 Frank noted that Phillip was back at work as a mental nurse, based at the Strathmont Hospital. Meanwhile Frank and Geri were travelling Europe in pursuit of Geraldine's ambitions to be a singer of renown, flitting between 'the smog of Milan' and 'the fresh air of Antwerp'. Rosemary and Melvyn paid periodic visits from Melbourne, bringing the Hackett Jones' two young grandchildren, Rachel and Francesca, and sometimes a cold virus too. Frank had always found lung and throat infections to be more threatening than did most people.[23]

Frank Senior's only full brother, the ageing Sydney medico Allan Hackett-Jones, also paid a visit during May of 1972.

Frank had, almost subconsciously, always felt some resentment that his sickly younger brother had attracted so much of their mother's attention and affection. Their father, Charles Firman Jones, himself the product of a love-starved domestic situation, probably resented the mother being distracted from wifely responsibilities by either of his younger sons. The emotional deprivations of childhood relationships contributed to Frank placing a high value on his own wife.[24]

In the mid-1970s the international exploits of the eldest son Frank and his singing wife Geraldine continued to take up more space in Frank's letters to Alfred Gardner than did the doings of any of the other children. They had recently spent a ten-week holiday in Australia, and returned to England at the end of August, 1974. The father seemed concerned that Frank Jr worked very long hours, and was overweight. He further noted, without comment, that his eldest son had a share in a light aeroplane, and had flown it around Adelaide and Kangaroo Island. Given the father's attitude to automobiles, he probably had very mixed feelings about infernal machines that floated perilously so far above the ground. Frank Sr indicated even deeper concern about Geraldine, who appeared to be abandoning her singing aspirations, as her career plans in Europe seemed not to be coming to fruition in the way she and Frank Jr had hoped. Geraldine was expecting a child, in due course named Alasdair, and she was then adjusting to life as the mistress of a 'three-storey picturesque house and grounds' (a century-old vicarage) just outside Cambridge in distant England. Frank visualised his daughter-in-law in that exotic and distant situation, surrounded by books and pictures and rose gardens, in which she walked her two large dogs. It was a setting far separated from the prosaic environs of a long-serving New South Wales public servant and small-time Adelaide lawyer.

The ageing Adelaide man was concerned that Geraldine wished to stay on in an England that offered shrinking commercial opportunities, and that his eldest son's career prospects (that loomed larger with the daughter-in-law's abandonment of her aspirations for a singing career) were endangered. Frank Jr had previously declined an attractive promotion offer in the interests of his wife's singing ambitions. That offer might have taken him to Connecticut in the United States, and his father worried that the eldest son might now be forced to take a position somewhere even less suited to his wife's inclinations. He told Alfred Gardner that 'we are doing our best to find jobs here for which he could apply'. Frank Jr solved his problem by going into business on his own account, and from very small beginnings he achieved rapid success as a supplier and manufacturer of sophisticated telecommunications equipment in Europe (eventually in Australia too). However, as his father had feared, that marriage relationship that had been strained by widely divergent career opportunities and demands did not long survive.[25]

Frank Sr's Adelaide garden helped him to get away from parental worries about the ever-varied activities of his maturing family. In April 1972 he wrote of the good weather, 'typical of drought', and his stern battle against the ravages of red spider mite. He had plenty of lettuce, tomatoes, and butter beans maturing rapidly under that intense Adelaide sun. His beans were coming in, and onions, red beet, carrots, and kohl rabi were well on the way. His one complaint to Alfred Gardner was that 'your climbing beans insist on bearing their fruit at the top of my tennis court fence; I must grow them on something lower'. At eighty years of age, the prospect of climbing ladders to the top of the tennis court fence in search of beans had no attraction. In later years, that tennis court was gradually assimilated into Frank's garden and orchard area.[26]

In the summer of 1974 Alfred Gardner was again being regaled with accounts of the productivity of that Adelaide vegetable garden. Wife Mary was holding up her end of the partnership as one reared in the country: 'Mary has made a number of bottles of grape juice and numerous bottles of preserved tomatoes and tomato sauce'. Apart from the white butterflies whose voracious larvae plagued his broccoli and cabbages, all was well in the Adelaide garden; and fruit trees were growing rapidly on the old tennis court to provide juicy eating for Frank's ninth decade. The threat posed by the abominable fruit fly, of which threatening vermin three had been trapped in the garden during that January, appeared to have dissipated. Those agricultural leanings that had been inherited from his rural youth provided a healthy outlet during Frank Hackett-Jones' latter years in the friendly dry heat of an Adelaide summer. In these advancing years he became increasingly dependent on the physical assistance of paid gardeners, but commented to his friend that 'I do enough walking around the garden'.[27]

Mary Hackett-Jones had inherited enough of her mother's disposition that taking an interest in the welfare of people had more attraction than the bottling of orchard or garden produce. With her own large brood having reached a state of adult independence, she looked for others (apart from her ageing husband and her grandchildren) who could benefit from her care. Mary became an elder of the Uniting Church for six years, until the increasing pressure of looking after her ailing husband produced a heart attack. During the 1980s Mary and Frank acted as sponsors for a Vietnamese family with four children, who were struggling to adapt to Australian ways in Adelaide. The father had been a teacher in Hong Kong, and Mary went over to collect them from the 'little tin shed' that served as a transit home for immigrants. Frank also took an interest, attempting to teach the immigrant family some basic English. He had, after all, started his working life before World War I as a school teacher; and he found far more gratitude for the efforts of his old age, than he had experienced as a Sydney primary school teacher long before.

Frank and Mary prepare for a portrait, Adelaide circa 1982.

In the context of the increasing strain of looking after her own ageing and ailing husband, the effort to communicate with a family that spoke virtually no English and helping to introduce them to the ways of a new land made Mary very tired. However, the gratitude and determination to succeed of the 'newly-adopted' Asian family in their new homeland provided much satisfaction to the Hackett-Jones family, who rapidly developed a deep respect for their Asian friends. Mary was shocked when the father of this immigrant family died of cancer at the age of only thirty-eight, but was happy that the wife and family continued to flourish in their new environment.

In 1987 this author visited Frank and Mary in Adelaide, in order to ascertain how Frank himself understood the outlines of his life story. For the earlier part of that pilgrimage, prior

Mary and Frank with baby Michael, 1980

Mary and Frank on their front veranda, Adelaide

to his marriage in 1939, Frank had previously committed a skeleton outline to writing. Being a very private person, he had many reservations about the idea of other family members that his life story should become the subject of a book. Frank was not interested in discussing any aspect of his personal or domestic life. All that he was really prepared to talk about was the considerable variety of working roles in which he had at some time been engaged, as well as his latter-day religious crusades in Adelaide. Frank made it clear that his own personality had been seriously and adversely affected by the tactics of revivalist preachers during his childhood, and (possibly because of my own theological background) was keen to share critical letters that he had written to various Protestant ministers throughout the 1960s and 1970s.

Frank volunteered very little information about his own father or mother, just as in his own childhood his father's parents had never been spoken of. Probably because of emotional deprivation in his own youthful domestic environment, Frank regarded the area of human relationships as something akin to sacred, and therefore taboo for biographical purposes. The man who had many years before used a telephone as the medium through which to propose to his chosen bride was not about to let any cats out of the bag of his life's more intimate secrets.

Frank insisted that he have the right to vet any manuscript that might arise from those Adelaide interviews. He appeared more concerned that the manuscript might embarrass members of his immediate family, than concerned about what it might say about him. That vetting of the manuscript was not to be, because it was not possible at that time to pursue the many but undetailed clues on Frank's past that had been gleaned over one week in Adelaide. I strongly doubt whether Frank could have accepted any other person's attempts to make sense of his life's complex pattern. He had his own strong and clear ethical perspective, and a barrister's impatience with statements that were not solidly based on the sort of evidence acceptable in a court of law. Readable biography cannot be written within the limits of those constraints.

Any biography must to a considerable extent gain its unity from the consistency of application of the author's own particular values. However, this author has attempted to adhere largely to Frank Hackett-Jones' own skeletal outline of what his life's story should be. Despite Frank's great precision of mind, and his ever-bubbling ironic wit, his own autobiographical outline as committed to writing was basically chronicle: a bare list of facts arranged according to dates. The one exception was his treatment of the World War I phase, where the heightened emotional intensity of that significant epoch of Frank's youth periodically broke through the bare factual outline. However, there would be no possibilities of libel suits arising from anything that Frank Hackett-Jones wrote or spoke about his past.

At that stage Frank was 95 years old, and a diagnosis of cancer had made it obvious that his life's pilgrimage was nearing its completion. Characteristically, he was not indicating concern about his own situation except insofar as it affected others close to him. With his usual thoroughness and clarity of mind, Frank struggled to ensure that his wife should be securely set up in appropriate home-unit accommodation before his death. That process cost him considerable anxiety, as he energetically pursued discomforting rumours that the desired accommodation might have serious structural defects. Although his much-battered body was fast giving out, Frank was not about to opt out of what had long been accepted as his responsibilities as head of the house. That highly disciplined mind, early shaped by the rigorous demands of an accountant's and a barrister's training, remained allied to a strong will and a clear vision of ethical responsibility of which Professor Samuel Angus of Sydney University could have been proud. So much so, that at times his long-time devoted wife and nurse clearly indicated her frustration, and a wish that the very aged and sick man should relax his hold on the reins of control and leave the thinking and worrying to others.

Frank struggled on long enough to move with Mary into an attractive new home unit overlooking Adelaide's parklands. Mary, who long shared with her husband a deep suspicion of the use of alcohol in human society, smiled about the couple of bottles of whisky that were brought into the home to lighten the burden of Frank's latter-day pain and anxieties. She never actually saw it being consumed, but noted that it somehow disappeared. When it became obvious that the end was close, Frank expressed a wish to speak by telephone to his eldest son Frank Jr who conducted his international telecommunications manufacture and supply business from Europe. Only when there was no alternative was Frank Hackett-Jones prepared formally to hand over responsibility for his family's well-being to his trusted and able eldest son.

A fair slab of Australian history must have died with the strong-willed and tight-lipped ninety-five-year-old veteran, but this book is the result of the wish of family members that Frank Hackett-Jones' very varied and unusually extensive life experience should have some permanent literary memorial. The research for this book could not have been undertaken without financial support from Frank Hackett-Jones Jr, and the manuscript would not have been published without continuing financial support from Frank's daughters. The record of our Australian past can hardly be the poorer for it.

Few ordinary Australians have books written about them, and middle class accountants, lawyers and public servants do not normally attract Australian historians, biographers or publishers as moths to a lamp. Biographers are generally reluctant to tackle a life story where the primary source materials and oral evidence left behind are as limited as in the present case. That is one reason why 'ordinary folk' seldom have books written about them. However, to attempt to understand the history of the past century on this strange southern continent without reference to the lives of such typical middle-class Australians of the Menzies era as Frank Hackett-Jones, is to participate in the perpetuation of a great Australian lie.

Frank and Mary's last portrait, Adelaide 1986

Frank with daughter Jennifer

Children of Frank Hackett-Jones, from top, l-r:
Frank Hackett-Jones with Rosemary, Phillip and
Frank, Richard, Geoffrey and Jennie

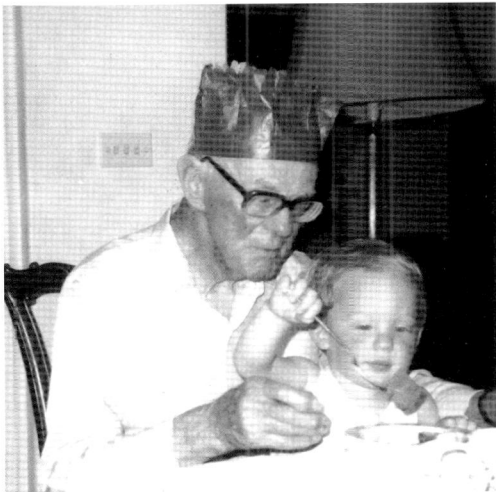

Grandchildren of Frank
Hackett-Jones, from top, l-r: Frank
Hackett-Jones with Angus, Rachel
with Francesca and Michael, Emily,
Mary, Angus and Marian, and
Alasdair with Frank Jr and Gaffer.

Bibliography

Angus, Samuel. *Truth and Tradition*. Angus & Robertson, Sydney, 1934.

Archives Office of New South Wales. *Reports of Vessels Arrived July 1826-1831*. Deakin University. Reel 1263. Colonial Secretary.

——. *Butts and Certificates of Publicans' Licences*. Treasury. Deakin University. Microfilm reel 5058.

——. *Clive Evatt Papers* (alphabetical by name/topic). 2/8201 and 2/8202.

——. *Convict Indents*, see ship *Surrey*, 1840. Deakin University. Microfilm.

——. *Early N.S.W. Baptismal Records*. La Trobe Library. Microfiche.

——. *Early Births, Deaths and Marriages in New South Wales*. La Trobe Library. Microfiche.

——. *Early N.S.W. Convict Marriage Banns and Marriages*. Deakin University. Microfiche.

——. *Index to Friendly and Co-operative Societies' Document Register, 1900-1910*. Kingswood, 7/6390; also 7/6364, index, 1911 on.

——. & Mitchell Library. *N.S.W. Public Service Lists*.

——. *Returned Soldiers' Settlement Act*. 3/2268, 1916.

Australasian Methodist Ministerial General Index, 1914.

Bean, C.E.W. & Gullett, H.S. *Photographic Record of the War*. vol. 12 of *The Official History of Australia in the War of 1914-18*. Angus & Robertson, Sydney, 1923.

Brookes, Mabel. *Riders of Time*. Macmillan, Melbourne, 1967.

Burke, Bernard. *The General Armory of England, Scotland, Ireland, and Wales*. Clearfield Press, London, 1884.

Burke, Bernard & Montgomery-Massingberd, Hugh. *Burke's Irish Family Records*. Burke's Peerage, London, 1976.

Census of the Commonwealth of Australia. vol. 1. Australian Bureau of Statistics, 30 June 1954.

Clark, Manning. *A History of Australia*. vol. 1. Melbourne University Press, 1962.

——. *Select Documents in Australian History 1788-1850*. Sydney, 1950.

——. *Select Documents in Australian History 1851-1900*. Sydney, 1955.

Coffey, H.W. & Morgan, M.J. *Irish Families in Australia and New Zealand 1788-1985, vol. 2: Eades-Lyttle*, rev. ed. South Melbourne, 1983.

Crowley, F.K. *Modern Australia in Documents, 1901-1939*. Wren, Melbourne, 1973.

——. *A New History of Australia*. Heinemann, Melbourne, 1974.

Cunningham, P.M. *Two Years in New South Wales*, vol. 1. Henry Colburn, London, 1827.

Cusack, D. & James, F. *Come In Spinner*. Angus & Robertson, Sydney, 1951.

Dunlop, E.W. 'The Public High Schools of New South Wales 1883-1912', *Royal Australian Historical Society Journal*.

Edmonds, Catherine Beatrice. *Caddie: a Sydney Barmaid*. Constable & Co., London, 1953.

Encyclopaedia Britannica. 9th ed., vol. 10. A&C Black, London 1878.

——. 12th ed., vol. 32. London and New York 1922.

GIBBNEY, H.J. & SMITH, A.G. *A Biographical Register 1788-1939, Notes from the name index of the Australian Dictionary of Biography.* vols 1 and 2. Australian Dictionary of Biography, Canberra, 1987.

GULLETT, H.S. *The Australian Imperial Force in Sinai and Palestine 1914-1918.* vol. 7 of *The Official History of Australia in the War of 1914-1918.* Angus & Robertson, Sydney, 1923.

HACKETT-JONES, ALAN. Collection of family birth, death and marriage certificates. Courtesy Mary Hackett-Jones, Adelaide.

——. Notes on ancestors. Courtesy Mary Hackett-Jones, Adelaide.

Hackett-Jones, Frank. Memoirs of his early life.

——. Letters to Alfred Gardner, 1963-1974. Courtesy Mary Hackett-Jones.

——. Letters to J.R. Lawrie, 27 June 1975. Courtesy Mary Hackett-Jones.

HUGHES, C.A. & GRAHAM, B.D. *A Handbook of Australian Government and Politics, 1890-1964.* ANU Press, Canberra, 1968.

JONES, M.A. *Housing and Poverty in Australia.* Melbourne University Press, 1972.

KELLY, V. *William McKell, a Man of the People: from Boilermaker to Governor-General; the Career of the Rt Hon Sir William McKell.* Alpha Books, 1971.

LANG, J.T. *I Remember.* Invincible Press, Sydney, 1956.

Letters of condolence on death of Rev. Mr Jones. Courtesy Mary Hackett-Jones, Adelaide.

Lexigraphical Index to All Passengers to Sydney, 1828-1842. Deakin University. Microfilm.

MacLYSAGHT, EDWARD. *Irish Families. Their Names, Arms and Origins.* Hodges Figgis, Dublin 1957.

The Methodist 1925.

NAIRN, B. *The 'Big Fella' Jack Lang and the Australian Labor Party 1891-1949.* Melbourne University Press, 1986.

NAIRN, B. & SERLE, G. *Australian Dictionary of Biography.* vol. 9, 1891-1939, Melbourne University Press, 1983.

New South Wales Government Gazette, 1919, 1922, 1924, 1928, 1930, 1942, 1943.

N.S.W. Methodist Conference Minutes 1925.

N.S.W. Parliamentary Papers 1941-1952.

New South Wales Year Book 1912.

Pastoral Times 1880-81.

Picturesque Atlas of Australasia. Andrew Garran, Sydney, 1886.

RADI, H., SPEARRITT, P. & HINTON, E. *Biographical Register of the New South Wales Parliament, 1901-1970.* ANU Press, Canberra, 1979.

RITCHIE, J. *Australia as Once We Were.* Heinemann, Melbourne, 1975.

ROBSON, LLOYD L. *The Convict Settlers of Australia.* Melbourne University Press, 1965.

SALT, A. *These Outcast Women: the Parramatta Female Factory 1821-1848.* Hale & Iremonger, Sydney, 1984.

SMITH, JAMES (ed.). *Cyclopaedia of Victoria.* Melbourne, 1903.

SPEARRITT, P. *Sydney's Century: a History,* UNSW Press, Sydney, 2000.

Sydney Gazette 1841-2.

Sydney Morning Herald 1842-46.

TENANT, K. *Evatt: Politics and Justice.* Angus & Robertson, Sydney, 1970.

TRIVETT, J.B. *New South Wales Friendly Societies' Experience, 1900-1908.* Sydney, 1910.

Victorian Government Gazette 1854-1864.

WADE, R.E. *The Methodists of Wagga Wagga and District.* Wagga Wagga Parish Council, 1980.

WALKER, R.B. *The Newspaper Press in New South Wales, 1803-1920.* Sydney University Press, 1976.

References

Chapter 1

[1] Allan Hackett Jones' collection of family birth, death and marriage certificates, courtesy of Mary Hackett-Jones, Adelaide.

[2] Lloyd Robson, *The Convict Settlers of Australia*, pp. 114 and 222.

[3] I am indebted to Deakin University's collection of microfilm convict sources, based on the records of the Archives Office of New South Wales (hereafter A.O.N.S.W.)

[4] A.O.N.S.W., Colonial Secretary, *Reports of Vessels Arrived July 1826-1831*, reel 1263, Deakin University; Certificate of Freedom no. 40/922, courtesy A.O.N.S.W.

[5] A.O.N.S.W., Butts and certificates of publicans' licences, Treasury, reel 5058, courtesy Deakin University, microfilm.

[6] *Encyclopaedia Britannica*, 9th ed., vol. 10, 1879, pp. 752-4.

[7] *Sydney Morning Herald*, 13 March 1846.

[8] *Lexigraphical Index to all Passengers to Sydney, 1828-1842*, courtesy Deakin University, microfilm.

[9] A.O.N.S.W., *Early Births, Deaths and Marriages in N.S.W.*, La Trobe Library, Melbourne, microfilm.

[10] *Lexigraphical Index*, see note 8 above.

[11] A.O.N.S.W., *Convict indents*, see ship *Surrey*, 1840, Deakin University, microfilm.

[12] *Sydney Morning Herald*, 23 Dec. 1842; early N.S.W. baptismal records, microfiche by A.O.N.S.W., consulted at La Trobe Library, Melbourne.

[13] A.O.N.S.W., Materials on early N.S.W. convict marriage banns, and on convict marriages, Deakin University, microfiche.

[14] Manning Clark, *A History of Australia*, vol. 1, p. 240.

[15] Manning Clark, *Select Documents in Australian History 1788-1850*, pp. 114-119.

[16] P. Cunningham, *Two Years in New South Wales*, vol. 1, p. 75.

[17] P. Cunningham, *Two Years in New South Wales*, vol. 1, p. 99.

[18] *Sydney Gazette*, 4 May 1841, p. 2.

[19] *Sydney Gazette*, 30 April 1842, p. 4.

[20] A.O.N.S.W., *Butts and certificates of publicans' licences*, reel 5058, Treasury, courtesy Deakin University, microfilm.

[21] Annette Salt, *These Outcast Women: The Parramatta Female Factory 1821-1848*, Sydney, 1984, p. 53 and p. 112.

[22] Alan Hackett-Jones' collection of family birth, death and marriage certificates, plus miscellaneous information on his ancestors, courtesy Mary Hackett-Jones, Adelaide.

[23] James Smith (ed.), *Cyclopaedia of Victoria*, Melbourne 1903, vol. 1, pp. 189-193.

[24] *Victorian Government Gazette*, 1864, vol. 2, p. 2407.

[25] *Burke's Irish Family Records*, London, 1976, pp. 536-40; Edward MacLysaght, *Irish Families. Their Names, Arms and Origins*, Dublin, 1978; *Burke's General Armory*, London, 1984, p. 438; Allan Hackett Jones' notes, courtesy Mary Hackett-Jones, Adelaide.

[26] H.J.Gibbney & A.G.Smith, *A Biographical Register 1788-1939*, vol. 1, A-K; *Victorian Government Gazette*, vol. 6, 1854, p. 312, vol. 7, 1854, p. 2259, vol. 12, 1856, p. 1659; *Australian Dictionary of Biography*, vol. 9, pp. 150-3

[27] H.W. Coffey & M.J. Morgan, *Irish Families in Australia and New Zealand 1788-1985*, vol. 2, p. 99.

[28] R.B. Walker, *The Newspaper Press in New South Wales, 1803-1920*, Sydney, 1976, p. 241; *Pastoral Times*, 31 Jan. 1880; *Australasian Methodist Ministerial General Index*, 1914, p. 32.

[29] *Picturesque Atlas of Australasia*, pp. 142-143.

[30] *Pastoral Times*, 27 March 1880, 7 February 1880.

[31] *Pastoral Times*, 23 April 1881.

[32] *Pastoral Times*, 27 March 1880.

[33] P. Geeves & James Jervis, *Rockdale: Its Beginning and Development*, Sydney, 1954, pp. 5-7, 48, 84, 104, 148.

[34] *Picturesque Atlas of Australasia*, pp. 103-105.

Chapter 2

[1] C.M.H. Clark, *Select Documents in Australian History 1851-1901*, Sydney, 1955, pp. 586-7; Frank Hackett-Jones, memoirs of his early life.

[2] *The Picturesque Atlas of Australasia*, pp. 122-3.

[3] *The Picturesque Atlas of Australasia*, p. 136 and 140 (lithograph of Kiama).

[4] Frank Hackett-Jones, memoirs of his early life.

[5] Frank Hackett-Jones, memoirs of his early life.

Chapter 3

[1] *Caddie: a Sydney Barmaid*, Sun Books, Melbourne, 1977, pp. 7-15.

[2] *New South Wales Year Book*, 1912, p. 94.

[3] E.W. Dunlop, 'The Public High Schools of New South Wales, 1883-1912', *Royal Australian Historical Society Journal*, vol. 51, March 1965, p. 73.

[4] *New South Wales Year Book*, 1912, p. 94; V. Kelly, *William McKell, Man of the People*, p. 13.

[5] Frank Hackett-Jones, memoirs of his early years.

[6] E.D. Dunlop, 'The Public High Schools of New South Wales, 1883-1912', *Royal Australian Historical Society Journal*, vol. 51, March 1965, p. 82; *New South Wales Year Book*, 1912, p. 86.

[7] F. Hackett-Jones, memoirs of his early years.

[8] K.Tenant, *Evatt, Politics and Justice*, Sydney, 1901, pp. 19-20.

[9] S. Piggott, *Dictionary of National Biography*, 1951-1960, Lond.1971, pp. 218-219; V. Kelly, *William McKell, Man of the People*, p. 22, pp. 36-7; K. Tennant, *Evatt*, pp. 20-21, p. 101, p. 356.

[10] *New South Wales Year Book*, 1912, p. 96.

[11] F. Hackett-Jones, memoirs of his early years.

[12] *Minutes of the New South Wales Methodist Conference*, 1925, p. 92.

[13] A.O.N.S.W. and Mitchell Library, *New South Wales Public Service Lists*, Sydney.

[14] *New South Wales Government Gazette*, no. 158, 1 Oct., 1913, p. 6055.

[15] C.A. Hughes and B. D. Graham, *A Handbook of Australian Government and Politics, 1890-1964*, Canberra, 1968, pp. 60-67

[16] F. Hackett-Jones, memoirs of his early years.

[17] J.B. Trivett, *New South Wales Friendly Societiesí Experience, 1900-1908*, Sydney, 1910, p. 7.

[18] J.B. Trivett, *New South Wales Friendly Societiesí Experience, 1900-1908*, p. 8.

[19] A.O.N.S.W. and Mitchell Library, *New South Wales Public Service Lists*, Sydney.

[20] *Bulletin*, 6 May, 1915, quoted in F. K. Crowley, *Modern Australia in Documents, 1901-1939*, Melbourne 1973, vol. 1, pp. 237-8.

[21] Frank Hackett-Jones, memoirs of his early years.

Chapter 4

[1] A.O.N.S.W. and Mitchell Library, *New South Wales Public Service Lists*, Sydney.

[2] *New South Wales, Government Gazette*, no. 158, 1 Oct., 1913, p. 6055.

[3] C.A. Hughes and B. D. Graham, *A Handbook of Australian Government and Politics, 1890-1964*, Canberra, 1968, pp. 60-67.

[4] J.B. Trivett, *New South Wales Friendly Societies' Experience, 1900-1908*, Sydney, 1910, p. 7; F. Hackett-Jones, memoirs of his early years, manuscript in possession of Mary Hackett-Jones, Adelaide.

[5] J.B. Trivett, *New South Wales Friendly Societies' Experience, 1900-1908*, p. 8.

[6] A.O.N.S.W. and Mitchell Library, *New South Wales, Public Service Lists*, Sydney.

[7] *Bulletin*, 6 May, 1915, quoted in F. K. Crowley, *Modern Australia in Documents, 1901-1939*, Melbourne 1973, vol. 1, pp. 237-8.

[8] Frank Hackett-Jones, memoirs of his early years.

[9] Harry Pirie-Gordon, 'Turkish Campaigns' (4), The Palestine Campaign, in *Encyclopaedia Britannica*, 12th Edition, vol. 32, London and New York, 1922, pp. 819-825.

[10] Frank Hackett-Jones, memoirs of his early years.

[11] Harry Pirie-Gordon, 'Turkish Campaigns' (4), The Palestine Campaign, in *Encyclopaedia Britannica*, 12th Edition, vol. 32, London and New York 1922, pp. 819-825; H.S. Gullett, *The Australian Imperial Force in Sinai and Palestine 1914-1918*, Sydney, 1923; C.E.W. Bean & H.S. Gullett, *Photographic Record of the War*, Sydney, 1923, pp. 641-2, 659, etc.

[12] Frank Hackett-Jones, memoirs of his early years.

[13] Dame Mabel Brooks, *Riders of Time*, Melbourne, 1967, pp. 213-217; H.S. Gullett, *The Australian Imperial Force in Sinai and Palestine 1914-1918*, Sydney, 1923.

[14] Frank Hackett-Jones, memoirs of his early years.

Chapter 5

[1] *New South Wales Government Gazette*, no. 136, 6 June, 1919, p. 2320.

[2] *New South Wales Government Gazette*, no. 258, 14 Nov. 1919, p. 6389; *New South Wales Public Service Lists*, 1919, p. 22; 1920, p. 19; 1921, p. 20.

[3] Frank Hackett-Jones, memoirs of his early life.

[4] A.O.N.S.W., Kingswood, 7/6390, *Index to friendly and co-operative societies' document register*, 1900-1910; 7/6364, index, 1911 on.

[5] *New South Wales Public Service Lists*, 1923, p. 70.

[6] V. Kelly, *William McKell, Man of the People*, p. 31.

[7] C.A. Hughes & B.D. Graham, *A Handbook of Australian Government and Politics, 1890-1964*, Canberra, 1968.

[8] *New South Wales Government Gazette*, 4 July 1922, p. 4446; 7 July 1922, p. 3761.

[9] Frank Hackett-Jones, memoirs of his early life.

[10] Archives Office of New South Wales, Kingswood, 3/2268, Returned Soldiers' Settlement Act, 1916.

[11] H. Radi, '1920-29', p. 361 of F.K. Crowley, *A New History of Australia*, Melbourne, 1974.

[12] J. Ritchie, *Australia as Once We Were*, Melbourne, 1975, pp. 199-206.

[13] A.O.N.S.W., Kingswood, 3/6470; *Government Gazette*, no. 104, 8 August 1924, p. 3982.

[14] Minutes of the New South Wales Methodist Conference for 1925; R. E. Wade, *The Methodists of Wagga Wagga and District*, Wagga Wagga, 1980, p. 83.

[15] *The Methodist*, 21 Feb. 1925, p. 3.

[16] Condolence letters, courtesy of Mary Hackett-Jones, Adelaide.

[17] P. Spearritt, *Sydney's Century: a History*, pp. 12-14.

[18] On Lang, see J.T. Lang, *I Remember*, Sydney, 1956; B. Nairn, *The 'Big Fella' Jack Lang and the Australian Labor Party 1891-1949*, Melbourne, 1986.

[19] State Archives of New South Wales, Kingswood, 7/6364, vol. 1.

[20] *New South Wales Public Service Lists*, 1928, p. 35; Frank Hackett-Jones, Memoirs of his early life.

Chapter 6

[1] *New South Wales Government Gazette*, no. 72, 13 June 1930, p. 2280.

[2] S. Angus, *Truth and Tradition*, Sydney, 1934, frontis.

[3] F. Hackett-Jones, Memoirs of his early years.

[4] F. Hackett-Jones, Memoirs of his early years.

[5] D. Cusack & F. James, *Come In Spinner*, Sydney, 1951.

[6] F. Hackett-Jones, Memoirs of his early years.

Chapter 8

[1] *New South Wales Parliamentary Papers*. 1945-46, vol. 1, pp. 298, 313, 315.

[2] P. Spearritt, *Sydney's Century: a History*, p. 75; V. Kelly, *William McKell, A Man of the People*, p 75.

[3] P. Spearritt, *Sydney's Century: a History*, pp. 15, 68, 69.

[4] P. Spearritt, *Sydney's Century: a History*, p. 75.

[5] P. Spearritt, *Sydney's Century: a History*, pp. 80-81.

[6] *New South Wales Parliamentary Papers*, 24 July 1941, 7 Oct. 1942, 29 July 1941.

[7] *New South Wales Parliamentary Papers*, 24 July 1941.

[8] *New South Wales Parliamentary Papers*, 23 July 1941.

[9] *New South Wales Government Gazette*, no. 150, 13 Nov. 1942, p. 2963.

[10] *New South Wales Government Gazette*, no. 143, 17 Dec. 43, p. 2195.

[11] P. Spearritt, *Sydney's Century: a History*, pp. 51-2.

[12] *New South Wales Parliamentary Papers*, 1945-46, vol. 1, pp. 304, 313.

[13] *New South Wales Parliamentary Papers*, 1947-48, vol. 1, p. 424.

[14] Information supplied by F. Hackett-Jones.

[15] New South Wales Parliamentary Papers, 1948-49-50, vol. 1, p. 19 (index), and references therein.

[16] V. Kelly, *William McKell, A Man of the People*.

[17] *New South Wales Parliamentary Papers*, 1945-46, vol. 1, p. 313; 1947-48, vol. 1, pp. 429-30 and 436-7.

[18] P. Spearritt, *Sydney's Century: a History*, pp. 101-2 and p. 68.

[19] Convenient rent tables for 1945-51, *New South Wales Parliamentary Papers*, 1950-51-52, vol. 3, p. 88.

[20] M.A. Jones, *Housing and Poverty in Australia*, Melbourne, 1972, p. 61.

[21] A.O.N.S.W., 2/8201 and 2/8202, Clive Evatt Papers (arranged alphabetically by name/topic) 'McHarg'.

[22] *New South Wales Parliamentary Papers*, 1948-49-50, vol. 1, pp. 776 and 758.

[23] *New South Wales Parliamentary Papers*, 1948-49-50, vol. 1, pp. 781-2.

[24] *New South Wales Parliamentary Papers*, 1950-51-52, vol. 3, p. 37.

[25] *New South Wales Parliamentary Papers*, 1950-51-52, vol. 3, pp. 81-2.

[26] H. Radi, P. Spearritt & E. Hinton, *Biographical Register of the New South Wales Parliament*, 1901-1970, Canberra, 1979, pp. 88-9; K. Tenant, Evatt, p. 319.

[27] V. Kelly, *William McKell, Man of the People*, p. 103.

[28] Information from F. Hackett-Jones.

[29] A.O.N.S.W., 2/8202, *Clive Evatt Papers* (arranged alphabetically by me/topic) 'Zenfel'.

[30] A.O.N.S.W., 2/8202, 'Seidler'; 2/8202, 'McGirr'.

[31] A.O.N.S.W., 2/8201, 'Press'.

[32] M.A.Jones, *Housing & Poverty in Australia*, Melbourne 1972, p.82.

[33] Census of the Commonwealth of Australia, 30th June 1954, vol. 1, p. 69.

[34] New South Wales Parliamentary Papers, 1948-49-50, vol. 1, p. 759.

[35] *New South Wales Parliamentary Papers*, 1942-43, vol. 1, p. 237, Estimates.

[36] *New South Wales Parliamentary Papers*, 1944-45, vol. 1, p. 235, Estimates.

Chapter 9

[1] This section depends heavily on information supplied by Frank and Mary Hackett-Jones, and by members of their family.
[2] Letter to Alfred Gardner, 20 Feb. 1964.
[3] Letter to Alfred Gardner, 5 Mar. 1964.
[4] Letter to Alfred Gardner, 8 Sept. 1965.
[5] Letter to Alfred Gardner, 8 Sept. 1965.
[6] Letter to Alfred Gardner, 8 Sept. 1965.

Chapter 10

[1] Letter to Alfred Gardner, 9 Sept. 1963.
[2] Letter to Alfred Gardner, 9 Sept. 1963.
[3] Letter to Alfred Gardner, 16 March 1966.
[4] Letter to Alfred Gardner, 15 Feb. 1974.
[5] Letter to Alfred Gardner, 16 Sept. 1966.
[6] Letter to Alfred Gardner, 24 July 1967; 7 Nov. 1971.
[7] Letter to Alfred Gardner, 5 Oct. 1971.
[8] From an undated document (copy of a letter?) in F. Hackett-Jones' files, Adelaide.
[9] From an undated document (copy of a letter?) in F. Hackett-Jones' files, Adelaide.
[10] Letter to Alfred Gardner, 10 Sept. 1972; letter to J. R. Lawrie, 27 June 1975.
[11] Letter to J.R. Lawrie, 27 June 1975.
[12] Letter to J.R. Lawrie, 27 June 1975.
[13] Letter to J.R. Lawrie, 27 June 1975.
[14] Letter to Alfred Gardner, 5 Oct. 1971.
[15] Letter to Alfred Gardner, 15 Oct. 1974; also, 26 July 1971, and 15 Feb. 1974.
[16] Letter to Alfred Gardner, 15 Apr. 1974, 15 Feb. 1974.
[17] Letter to Alfred Gardner, 10 Sept. 1972.
[18] Letter to Alfred Gardner, 15 Feb. 1974; 7 May 1972.
[19] Letter to Alfred Gardner, 16 Sept. 1966 and 30 July 1969.
[20] Letter to Alfred Gardner, 25 May 1971; 7 July 1971; 5 Oct. 1971
[21] Letter to Alfred Gardner, 24 June 1967; 26 July 1971, 6 Sept. 1971.
[22] Letter to Alfred Gardner, 26 July 1971.
[23] Letter to Alfred Gardner, 5 Oct. 1971; 10 Sept. 1972.
[24] Letter to Alfred Gardner, 7 May 1972.
[25] Letter to Alfred Gardner, 21 Sept. 1974.
[26] Letter to Alfred Gardner, 17 Apr. 1972.
[27] Letter to Alfred Gardner, 15 Feb. 1974.

Index